Live Your Life to the Fullest

Tunji Ishola

Dedication

The book of life says "Favour is deceitful, and beauty is in vain but a woman that fears the Lord, she shall be praised." I dedicate this book to my best friend, companion, confidant, lover and wife, whose sacrificial love is beyond description. Bisi, I declare to the whole world that you are the finest creature of God I have ever seen.

Thank you for being the best for me and your effort in making sure that I become the best in all I do. Love you MD.

Above all, my gratitude goes to God, the maker of life in whose breath I live and have my being.

Acknowledgements

I would like to thank and appreciate my parents Mr. and Mrs. Ishola for their love and sacrifice in raising me and equipping for the future ahead. Only God can reward you for the life's teaching you gave me and the confidence I found in you. I am grateful for my sister, Toyin and my brothers, Kola and Ope. My gratitude goes to my in-laws, the Olaopa's family, Mrs. Olaopa, Mrs. Dolly, Femi, Segun, Tobi and Toluwani.I am forever grateful for my uncle and the whole of Bello's family. God will reward your kindness shown to me.

They say it takes more than a village to raise a boy. I am forever grateful for the impact and generosity of Elder Segun and Pastor (Mrs.) Ayonrinde in my life and family. My heartfelt gratitude goes to the Oyekunle's family, Bakare's family, Odejide's family, Ogunlowo's family, Adeyemi's family. Thank you for your help and support at different stages of my life. Thanks for your encouragement. I am grateful for all my friends who stood by me when the going was tough, Tolu Ogunlowo, Abayomi Obembe, David Ogunniyi, Leye Ogundiran, Tunde Odejide, Sidney Sanni, Emmanuel Shidali and the late Eric Atisso. You guys are rare gem in my life.

I am eternally grateful for Rev Ayoola Olubusuyi and the whole family of Kingdom Life Christian Centre, Nigeria for your impacts and love. I am grateful for my pastor, Dr. Albert Odulele, Glory House, London. I am grateful for Rev. Vincent Odulele. Thank you for very much.

This page will not be complete without acknowledging the sacrifice and the sefless love of people in my life. These are people who out of their busy schedules decided to run with the vision of God for my life. You are the strength and the push behind "Lightspring International".

Thank you very much James Ogiemudia, Bunmi Bello, Tosin Gbadebo; Wunmi Ajayi, Ayo Taylor, Hannah Demuren, Michael Ekundayo and David Eto. You guys are my mighty men of valour. Thank you very much.

I am very grateful for all your invaluable assistance.

Contents

Introduction

We have all been blessed in a most unique and spectacular way with the best and most valuable gift at birth. This gracious gift has nothing to do with our ethnicity, gender, race, nationality or any other limiting factors, self-imposed or those we allowed others to impose on us.

Some do realise this gift early, while the vast majority of people are still chasing after the wind in search of this indescribable jewel of value. The discovery, development and the deployment of this gracious gift is the secret to true happiness and fulfilment.

When a person discovers and walks in the consciousness of this gift, such a person lightens his or her world with light as if by magic. Anything that comes along this path of light expresses fullness of relevance.

This gracious gift is called **"LIFE"**. This life is the summation of years, months, days, minutes and seconds expressed in day to day struggles and triumphs that are experienced by all of the world's creatures. It contains the possibility that exceeds human imagination and limitation. It is the wellspring of unlimited joy. It carries the seeds of greatness and unlocks treasures of eternal pleasures. The release of this life leads to extreme success in all endeavours. In it resides abundant living that unlocks doors to prominence and relevance.

Just A Minute **by Benjamin E. Mays**
I have only just a minute, only 60 seconds in it,

Forced upon me, can't refuse it.
Didn't seek it, didn't choose it,
But it's up to me to use it.
I must suffer if I lose it,
Give account if I abuse it,
Just a tiny little minute,
But eternity is in it.

What are you going to do with your greatest gift - **LIFE?** If there is ever going to be history written about you, you are already writing it now with the way you are using this wonderful gift of life.

This book is written to inspire those who are yet to discover the meaning of life, to help those who are in transition of becoming the best in all they do and to ignite a sense of legacy in those who are at the pinnacle of their race of life. This book embraces simplicity for easy understanding and to empower readers to turn their wishbone to backbone with the intent of growing and thriving in life's challenges instead of going through them.

It is possible to be more and do more!

YES, Life Is Tough!

Yes, life is tough! This was my response to one of my friends who just came out from an ordeal that almost made him give up on his dreams and passions. He spent hours giving me reasons and validated excuses why the journey was not worth pursuing. Fortunately for him, I just finished a book written by Willie Jolley – *It Only Takes A Minute To Change Your Life*. This book contains the story of a remarkable man called William Mitchell.

W Mitchell, The Man Who Would Not Die!

W Mitchell is a man who exemplifies overcoming life's obstacles.

He is respectfully called "the man that would not die."

Thirty years ago, Mitchell was a student who worked part time as a cable operator in San Francisco. Between school and work, he found time to ride his new Harley-Davidson motorcycle for recreation. He lived for times when he could get out on his bike and feel the refreshing wind blow on his face. One day while taking a ride, he was crossing an intersection and suddenly saw a truck running a red light. The truck slammed into Mitchell. He was knocked to the ground and as he laid there in agony he smelled gas and realised that he was covered with it.

Suddenly, there was an explosion and the bike went up in flames, and then the fire spread and soon engulfed Mitchell. He became a human torch and was completely burned from head to toe.

He lost his fingers and toes and was left with no resemblance to his former self. He went through months and months of agonising surgery and rehabilitation, but he never gave up.

He finished his education and went on to start a business that soon became successful. In fact, he was able to purchase a private plane that he piloted. His plane became his passion and he spent all of his spare time flying.

One evening, while in flight, the plane started experiencing engine problems. He attempted to land but lost control and crashed. When he awoke after months in coma, he found that now he was paralysed from the waist down! He sat and looked at himself and saw a burned man who was now paralysed and forced to live his life in a wheelchair.

Others expected him to give up, but Mitchell refused. He said "there used to be ten thousand things that I could do; now there are nine thousand."

He went on to share his story with others and has become one of the top motivational speakers in the world. He owns homes in Colorado, California and Hawaii. He truly lives the life to the fullest. He lives the life that he talks about. It is not what happens to you that counts. It is what you do about it.

As you go through the pages of this book, you will come across principles and stories of people referred to as **"extremely successful people"** who lived their lives by developing certain admirable qualities that singled them out of the crowd and made them a cynosure of all eyes.

It is my earnest heartfelt prayer that as we also develop these qualities in line with the fear of God and step out to be our best, this world and the coming generation will never remain the same.

Tunji Ishola

CHAPTER ONE

Character – Part I

In the fifth century B.C., Heraclitus taught this timeless truth, "Character is destiny." It is a simple truth to be sure, but do not be fooled by its simplicity. Whether we lead lives that are destined to become richer, or poorer, depends entirely upon our character.

What is character? Dwight L. Moody, world-renowned 19th century American evangelist, answered that question, "Character is what you are in the dark."

Character is what determines what kinds of goals we will set and achieve, whether we will be honest or dishonest in dealing with others, and whether we will value and obey the rules of God and society even when no one is looking. Character is a set of behaviours that defines precisely who and what we are.

Character forms because of the choices we make. Even those choices that seem small and insignificant are choices that inevitably change us from who we are now into who we will become. In the words of Helen Douglas, "Character isn't inherited. One builds it daily by the way one thinks and acts, thought by thought, action by action."

Moreover, there is never a time when our excursion into character development ceases; we move either forward or backward in the development of our character, we never stand still. Character development is a never-ending journey, and the only meaningful question concerning it is the direction in which we are travelling.

Our character reflects what we think about ourselves, what we believe in strongly, and what we value above all else. The Bible teaches, "As a man thinks in his heart, so does he become." In other words, our deepest and most heartfelt beliefs, whether true or false, form a foundation for living; an underpinning that determines how we will act, the decisions we will make, and the friends with whom we will associate.

The study of character, therefore, is without doubt one of the most important studies upon which an individual can embark. Endeavouring to understand your own character, the elements that contribute to it, and recognising what you can do to shape and mould it, helps overcome the greatest obstacle that stands in the way of your success: yourself.

Character is foundational. A winning character is the very core of the formation of a successful life. If you truly want to lead a successful life, developing a winning character is the starting point. Of the characteristics that extremely successful people have in common, excellence of character is first on the list. It is no accident that character is the subject of the first chapter of this book.

Keep Your Eye on Your Destination

While the journey can sometimes be difficult, the destination is clearly worthwhile. Positive character traits lead to the achievement of goals; and the achievement of goals leads to success in life. Negative character traits have but one destination, failure.

Positive character traits lead to successful relationships and will open you to the possibility of continued rewards. Conversely, others are likely to respond to you with distrust, even dislike, if you allow negative character traits to dominate your life.

Positive character traits that involve obeying the rules even when nobody is looking define a person as trustworthy, law-abiding, and a model citizen. This kind of person is a leader, a role model, and an outstanding member of any group with which he is affiliated.

Those who possess negative character traits often do not follow the rules, in public or in private, and are labeled law-breakers, troublemakers, or sinners. Their character is immoral, unethical, or corrupt.

How you choose to define and fashion your character will have more to do with your success, or failure, than another other single factor. Your character is more vital than intelligence, educational achievement, family wealth, appearance, or a hundred and one other features too often mistaken for the road to success in life.

Character embraces several fundamental qualities:

Attitude before Altitude

Attitude is the way in which you view the world around you. It is how you view yourself, your loved ones, your friends, your environment, and your future. It is the way you look at life.

Attitude is an essential component in character development. Attitude, not aptitude, determines whether you will strive to build a successful character, or shrink from the challenge altogether.

Charles R. Swindoll one of the greatest preachers of all time once wrote, "The longer I live, the more I realise the impact of attitude on life.

"Attitude, to me, is more important than facts. It is more important than the past, the education, the money, than circumstances, than failure, than successes, than what other people think or say or do. It is more important than appearance, giftedness or skill. It will make or break a company... a church... a home.

"The remarkable thing is we have a choice every day regarding the attitude we will embrace for that day. We cannot change our past . . . we cannot change the fact that people will act in a certain way. We cannot change the inevitable. The only thing we can do is play on the one string we have, and that is our attitude.

"I am convinced that life is 10% what happens to me and 90% how I react to it, and so it is with you . . . we are in charge of our attitudes."

In a recent Harvard University study, researchers found that employers hire people because of their attitude 85% of the time. Intelligence, specialized knowledge and degrees only account for about 15% of new hires.

If your goal is to lead a successful life in every sense of the term –a life that is rich with meaning and purpose – a winning attitude is an absolute must. You will never rise higher than your attitude allows. For you, developing a winning attitude, and making a personal commitment to maintain that attitude every day of your life, is not an option, it is an absolute necessity. A winning attitude and a positive approach to life are the bedrocks of your ultimate success.

A winning attitude determines your mood. It motivates you to move forward in your quest to achieve your goals and objectives. It inspires you to forward thinking "out of the box." It turns on the lights in your world and as if by magic connects you to opportunities that others miss.

A winning attitude keeps you focused on a positive future, especially during times of trial and uncertainty. It helps you pull yourself up by the bootstraps when life deals you a hefty blow, and it provides you with a true north when you occasionally lose your way.

Those who lack a winning attitude sometimes attain success, but they are unable to sustain it very long. A Positive attitude attracts success like a magnet. A negative attitude repels everything in its path.

Attitude is a lifestyle. Each day of your life, you can decide what kind of attitude will prevail. There are things in life you cannot change, no matter how hard you try. For example, you cannot change the past, nor can you change the future. You cannot change the attitudes of others, nor can you hold yourself responsible for their outcomes. However, you can change your attitude by a simple act of your will.

In the words of Samuel Johnson, ". . . he who has so little knowledge of human nature as to seek happiness by changing anything but his own disposition, will waste his life in fruitless efforts and multiply the grief he proposes to remove."

Attitude determines outcome; it gives you the winning edge in every situation you encounter. It is an important, but often ignored, key to success. People who find themselves in "failure mode" seemingly not able to succeed at anything in life should first consider their attitude. "Failure mode" is just another term for poor attitude. Change your attitude and you will change your life.

The words of Thomas Jefferson are just as true today as they were when he penned them centuries ago, "You are not what you think you are. You are what you think. Nothing can stop the person with the right mental attitude from achieving his (or her) goals. Nothing on earth can help the person with the wrong mental attitude."

Wayne Cordeiro is senior pastor of New Hope Christian Fellowship in Honolulu, one of the USA's fastest-growing churches. He is also the president of New Hope International, a ministry dedicated to developing emerging leaders to plant twenty-first-century churches. In his book *Attitudes That Attract Success*, Cordeiro says, "The Sermon on the Mount – perhaps Jesus' most famous sermon – addresses our attitudes. Theologians have called this series of teachings the 'Beatitudes'. I guess His lesson could be summed up this way: 'Your attitudes will determine what you will be.' Hence the Be-attitudes."

Finally, understand that those you encounter, spontaneously reflect your attitude back to you. Your attitude towards someone determines his or her attitude toward you. A smile usually begets a smile; a frown begets a frown. This law of attitudinal reciprocity is immutable. In other words, you will get what you give or in the words of St. Paul, "Whatsoever a man sows, that shall he also reap."

Attitude Formation

While other factors occasionally play a role, three major spheres of life account for most attitude formation. Social scientists often refer to these as three E's: Experience, Environment, and Education.

Experience

We have all heard the adage, "experience is the best teacher." It is true that one of the primary ways that humankind learns is from experience. A child, warned against touching a hot stove, burns herself when she disobeys. An adult who enjoys driving faster than the posted limit receives a citation and learns that speeding is a costly habit. A wife discovers that her loving husband has had an affair with a woman half her age and decides to end the marriage. The experience of losing the true love of his life teaches the husband an important lesson in fidelity and self-control, albeit too late.

In a very similar way, we learn to select positive or negative attitudes because of our past, present and future experiences. Ignorance and conditioning are the usual filters we use in deciding what kind of attitude we will embrace toward a specific experience. However, we are always free to choose a positive attitude if we want positive results to continue to dominate our lives.

We cannot often determine the experiences we will encounter in life, but we can control how we react to them; we can decide what our attitude will be concerning them. By constant reinforcement within ourselves of positive viewpoints and mental processes, we can remain positive even when confronted with issues that most would consider devastating. Being laid-off, or even terminated, are potentially positive experiences. Even death, separation, and loss have their positive aspects if you just think about it.

Negative experiences will always carry with them the seeds of negative attitude, and allowing those seeds to take root and grow in your mind means you will be developing a destructively negative attitude that will simply bring about more experiences that are negative.

However, by seeking out the good in every situation – by continuing to surround yourself with positive people and circumstances – you will attract more experiences that are positive. The choice is yours alone, but make it carefully. It is a choice with long-term consequences.

Environment

For years, social scientists have debated the competing influences of Nature and Nurture in the development of the human character. Some claim the idea that the influence of genetically transmitted characteristics predominately determines the human character. Others claim that the social environment – contact with other people – is the most important factor.

Today most social scientists agree that the development of human character involves a blending of heredity and social environmental influences, with environmental influences having the greatest significance.

In other words, if the people who surround you during your early years are negative and have bad attitudes about most things (family of origin, brothers, sisters, friends, classmates) chances are you will reflect that same negativity to others and, in turn, constantly draw negativity into your daily life.

As children, we do not have the ability to choose our parents, relatives, or brothers and sisters, or those who regularly interact with our families of origin, and have only a limited ability to determine the social community outside the home where we will spend much of our time (school community, friends, neighbours, etc.).

However, all of that changes when we become adults. As adults, we can choose the communities that will influence our lives. We can elect to surround ourselves only with those who have positive attitudes, are hardworking, focused and forward-thinking, or we can choose to continue to carry the baggage we were provided in our formative years, which for many of us is relatively negative (no pun intended).

It is your choice whether to draw negativity into your daily life by being negative, or start each day with a positive attitude and an expectation of success. You can chose to wish and dream about being a successful individual admired by everyone, or you can trade in your wishbone for a backbone and dare to approach life with a positive attitude knowing that you are on the road to success. It is all up to you.

However, if you choose be successful in life, do not forget the importance of surrounding yourself with successful, positive people. Developing that kind of a social community for yourself will help you maintain a positive attitude toward life and will keep you positively focused on your goals and objectives.

Education

Education takes two distinct forms: academic education, which involves the teaching of facts, theories, and skills; and values-based education that concerns itself with ethical and moral literacy. Both forms of education are essential, but one form without the other is downright dangerous.

Do not underestimate the value of a good academic education. A well-educated person will have prospects and opportunities that others simply will not have. The lifetime pay of a high school graduate compared to a dropout is significant; the same is true of a college graduate when compared to a high school graduate. Whether you consider it fair is not the point. It is a fact.

However, while a good academic education will help provide you with a good start in life, a values-based education is what is necessary to succeed greatly.

Values-based education usually begins in the home of our family of origin and continues as we grow spiritually and as we learn from others in our chosen social communities.

Values based education builds virtues like honesty, compassion, courage, and responsibility. I have never known an extremely successful person who possessed a solid academic education but lacked the virtues acquired through values-based education.

Just as attitude is linked to character, so too attitude is linked to education (both types). A bad attitude, therefore, is not only a sure sign that one's education has been neglected, it is also a signal of a major character flaw that needs to be fixed if extraordinary success is the goal.

The Formation of Bad Attitudes Begins Early

During childhood and adolescence, we build attitudes that will last a lifetime. Therefore, while it is never too late to begin changing your life by changing your attitudes, it is likewise never too early.

With the goal of combating bad attitudes before they are set in cement – attitudes that will surely set them up for certain failure - the richest man in the world, Bill Gates, addressed a group of High School students giving them the following eleven rules to live by:

Rule 1: Life is not fair - get used to it!

Rule 2: The world does not care about your self-esteem. The world will expect you to accomplish something before you feel good about yourself.

Rule 3: You will NOT make $60,000 a year right out of high school. You will not be a vice-president with a car phone until you earn both.

Rule 4: If you think your teacher is tough, wait until you get a boss.

Rule 5: Flipping burgers is not beneath your dignity. Your Grandparents had a different word for burger flipping: they called it opportunity.

Rule 6: If you mess up, it is not your parents' fault, so do not whine about your mistakes, learn from them.

Rule 7: Before you were born, your parents were not as boring as they are now. They got that way from paying your bills, cleaning your clothes and listening to you talk about how cool you thought you were. So before you save the rain forest from the parasites of your parent's generation, try delousing the closet in your own room.

Rule 8: Your school may have done away with winners and losers, but life has not. In some schools, they have abolished failing grades and they will give you as many times as you want to get the right answer. This does not bear the slightest resemblance to anything in real life.

Rule 9: Life is not divided into semesters. You do not get summers off and very few employers are interested in helping you find yourself. Do that on your own time.

Rule 10: Television is not real life. In real life, people actually have to leave the coffee shop and go to jobs.

Rule 11: Be nice to nerds. Chances are you will end up working for one.

Attitude is the Fountain of Youth

While we are on the subject of youth, let me direct you to an enduring truth about youthfulness. Some people live their entire lives searching for a "fountain of youth," something that will permit them to look and feel young. They usually give up in frustration, however, because the things they have tried eventually either failed or led them to frustration.

A positive attitude is the true fountain of youth! That is one of the world's most amazing secrets, and now it belongs to you. Share it with your family and friends.

Youth is not really a time of life; it is a state of mind, a product of the imagination and vigour of the emotions, a predominance of courage over timidity, an appetite for adventure. People do not grow old by living a certain number of years, they grow old when they desert their ideals, and no longer persist in achieving goals and objectives.

Years may wrinkle the skin, but to give up the pursuit of your dreams wrinkles your spirit.

Worry, self-doubt, fear, and anxiety – these are the culprits that bow the head and break the will.

Whether you are seventeen or ninety-seven, there exists in the heart of every person who loves life the thrill of a new challenge, the insatiable appetite for what is coming next. You are as young as your faith, and as old as your doubts.

So long as your heart receives from your head messages that reflect beauty, courage, joy, and excitement, you are young. When your thinking becomes clouded with pessimism and prevents you from taking risks and enjoying challenges, you are old.

How to Build a Positive Attitude

Here are some practical suggestions that will help you build a positive, life-changing attitude:

Believe in Optimism. Understand that a positive attitude (an attitude of optimism) will draw to your presence everything you need to succeed. Before you begin any project, understand that you will succeed, visualise it, and feel it. If there are set-backs along the way, your optimism will change these set-backs into stepping-stones to success; to the contrary, the pessimist (the person with the bad attitude) will see a set-back as an obstacle to success.

Adopt a Strong Work Ethic. Remember what Thomas Edison said, "Success is 1% inspiration, and 99% perspiration." A strong work ethic will reinforce your attitude with conviction and a sense of endurance.

Do It Now! Procrastination is the highway to failure because it is the direct route to a negative attitude. Think about it: a completed task on your way toward meeting a goal is satisfying, fulfilling, and even energising. An uncompleted task is draining and confirms to your innermost being that you will never succeed.

Live in the Now. It is always surprising to me that so many people live either in the past, or in the future. Living in the past is like trying to drive an automobile down the road with your eyes firmly fixed in the rear-view mirror; the result is certain to be devastating. Depression is generally the result. Conversely, living in the future is living in the unknown where there are a zillion questions about every possible situation in life, and each of the questions is the same: What if . . . ? Anxiety is usually the result of living in the future. Live in the here and now! That is the answer. By living in the present, you can deal with reality without the thieves of fear or self-judgement. Moreover, the present is all there is for you and me. The past and the future are only thoughts that are not subject to change no matter how hard we try. Every tool you need for success is in the here and now; God is in the here and now. Live for today.

Be Careful Of Your Associations. If you want to develop and maintain a positive attitude, surround yourself with people who possess positive attitudes. Stay away from the "negative Nellies" of this world, because they will drag you down to their level of life every time. It has been my experience that one's positive attitude very seldom influences a person with a negative attitude. On the other hand, a negative attitude will infect a positive attitude very quickly.

Develop a Love for Learning. The Bible tells us, "Knowledge is power," and that power helps you maintain a positive attitude in every situation in life. Read; fill your mind with the thoughts of great men who overcame incredible obstacles to achieve their dreams. Make it a habit to read for at least twenty minutes each day. In this way, by the end of one year, you will have read twenty, two hundred page books (18 more than the average reader will have read). Just think about the competitive advantage you will gain. Read self-help books, listen to tapes about character development and the importance of attitude; attend seminars that help people discover and maintain good attitudes. This is time well invested that will keep your attitude positive and pay enormous dividends as time goes by.

Focus on Your Strengths. Take inventory of yourself. What are your strengths? What are you good at doing? A positive attitude is reinforced by those who understand their strengths and use them to their advantage. Extremely successful people always focus on their strengths. Also-rans understand their strengths, but always focus on their weaknesses.

Accept Change. Life is constantly changing. In fact, change is the only thing in this world that is constant. Change with it. Examine the benefits that a change brings with it, accept them, and move on.

Do Not Blame Others. We live in a world that loves to play "the blame game." Those who live their lives with a negative attitude blame everything, and everyone but themselves for their failures. Do not be part of that. You are responsible for your success or failure, nothing or no one else. Take responsibility your failures and allow them to motivate you to begin again. Remember, winning the war is important; losing an occasional battle is simply something that takes place now and again in the process of winning the war.

Do Not Quit!
When things go wrong, as they sometimes will,
When the road you're trudging seems all uphill,
When the funds are low and the debts are high,
And you want to smile, but you have to sigh,
When care is pressing you down a bit,
Rest, if you must, but do not quit.
Life is queer with its twists and turns,
As every one of us sometimes learns,
And many a failure turns about,
When he might have won had he stuck it out;
Don't give up though the pace seems slow –
You may succeed with another blow.
Often the goal is nearer than,

It seems to a faint and faltering man,
Often the struggler has given up,
When he might have captured the victor's cup,
And he learned too late when the night slipped down,
How close he was to the golden crown.
Success is failure turned inside out-
The silver tint of the clouds of doubt,
And you never can tell how close you are,
It may be near when it seems so far,
So stick to the fight when you're hardest hit –
It's when things seem worst that you must not quit.
– Anonymous

The Primacy of Perseverance

Thomas Edison refused to give up when his first efforts to discover a filament for his carbon incandescent lamp failed. Edison continued his search by doing countless experiments with a variety of materials, but each failed. With each failure, Edison, perhaps out of pure frustration, tossed the worthless element out the window until the pile eventually reached the second story of his home.

Then, on October 13, 1879, after thirteen months of repeated failures, Edison finally succeeded in his search for a filament that would stand the stress of an electric current. His persistence against discouraging odds had given the world the wonder of the electric light bulb!

Perseverance is the commitment you make to yourself to do whatever is necessary to accomplish your most treasured dreams and goals. Perseverance means you refuse to give up in spite of the difficulty that may surround you and in spite of those who tell you that your goal is unattainable. Perseverance is a fundamental attribute of a winning character.

To accomplish something that is easy is something anyone can do. However, to accomplish that which is difficult – even seemingly impossible – is something that sets you apart.

History is replete with examples of men and women who have persevered in spite of the odds:

An editor once told **Louisa May Alcott**, author of *Little Women*, acclaimed as one of the best children's books ever written, that she would never write anything popular.

Even deafness could not stop **Ludwig Van Beethoven**. He composed many of his greatest works unable to hear the grandeur of the music he was creating.

At nineteen months of age, **Helen Keller** contracted a serious illness that left her blind and deaf. In spite of the odds being stacked against her, and with the help of her family and friends, she developed a winning character with a fierce sense of perseverance. She set herself apart from those with similar handicaps by refusing to give up and give in. She became the first blind and deaf person to earn a Bachelor of Arts degree, and ultimately became a prolific author, political activist, and lecturer.

A coach to former Angels' shortstop, **David Eckstein**, once told him that he would never play major college baseball. "That was hurtful but not defeating. I did not believe him. I was raised to believe in myself, so I just kept playing hard and giving 100%." A winning character, armed with perseverance, remains undaunted by the negative comments of others and simply continues moving forward toward the goal.

Jim Abbot, a former pitcher for the Angels enjoyed frustrating his cynics by continually proving them wrong. He overcame incredible odds and reached his goal of becoming a major league pitcher. He was born without a right hand.

Abraham Lincoln rose from a humble childhood on the

Indiana frontier to become the 16th President of the United States. Before his election in 1860 Lincoln had been a country lawyer, an Illinois state legislator, a member of the United States House of Representatives, and twice an unsuccessful candidate for election to the U.S. Senate.

His life is a testament to winning character and perseverance. "Honest Abe," as friend and foe affectionately labelled him, was largely self-educated. He was an avid reader and would sometimes walk several miles to borrow books in order to learn.

His accomplishments set him apart from the ordinary politician. He successfully led a fledgling country through its greatest internal crisis, the American Civil War, preserving the Union and ending slavery.

He overcame incredible odds to accomplish his goals including losing a son, suffering multiple illnesses, being plagued with frequent bouts of "melancholy" (clinical depression), and a host of betrayals by those in whom he had placed his great trust.

Albert Einstein, was slow in learning how to speak. In fact, his parents were so concerned about their child's lack of normal speech development that they consulted a physician. During Einstein's youth, one headmaster expelled him from school; another said that he would never amount to much. Nevertheless, Einstein persevered. Best known for his theory of relativity and specifically mass–energy equivalence, expressed by the equation $E = mc^2$ Einstein received the 1921 Nobel Prize in Physics "for his services to Theoretical Physics, and especially for his discovery of the law of the photoelectric effect." Today his name is synonymous with genius.

The List Goes On!

John F. Kennedy the 35th President of the United States had to take the New York bar exam three times before he passed.

Ray Charles, world-renowned musician and singer was blind.

Thomas Edison - had a learning problem.

James Earl Jones - had a speech impediment.

Franklin D. Roosevelt - was paralysed from polio

Itzhak Perlman - contracted polio at age four that left him paralyzed from the waist down.

Stevie Wonder- blind from birth.

Stephen Hawking - has amyotrophic lateral sclerosis (ALS), a condition that has progressed over the years and has left him almost completely paralysed.

Woodrow Wilson – suffered from dyslexia and was ten years of age before he learned to read. As a teenager he compensated for his handicap by teaching himself shorthand. His academic achievements were largely due to his absolute determination and self-discipline.

Terry Fox - diagnosed with osteosarcoma at age fifteen. His right leg was amputated several inches above the knee. Three years later, the young athlete decided to run from coast to coast in order to raise money for cancer research. His goal was to raise one dollar from each Canadian citizen.

Steps to Improving Your Perseverance

1. Don't Give Up! When you are working towards a goal and someone or something offers you an excuse to give up, say "NO." So many people are living lesser lives today than they could have if only they had not allowed someone or something to steal their dreams.

2. Overcome Fear with Faith. Do not let fear dictate who you are or what you are able to accomplish. Have faith in yourself; know that God has a plan for your life and that it is He who places opportunities in your life, fully expecting that you will make the most of them.

3. Learn from your Failures. Each of us experiences failures along life's journey. There is a reason for this: within every failure there is the seed of a lesson well learned. Each failure we experience reinforces an emerging solid character trait. It is our failures that contribute most intensely to our character development.

4. Welcome Difficult Times. Recent studies in psychology and biology, are confirming what our grandparents knew intuitively: exposure to difficult times makes us stronger, and psychologically more resilient. Here are some suggestions to consider for when difficult times arise: a) Focus on what you have, not on what you've lost; b) Do not be blinded by difficulty, search for opportunities that may exist as a result of the situation; c) Think about how you have been helped by the difficulty: how it has changed your personal values, what effect it has had on your relationships with your spouse and family members, how it has changed you spiritually; d) Think about the benefits of the event: perhaps you have rediscovered some personal values, or rediscovered a dream, or learned more about your mission and purpose in life; e) Consider how the circumstance has made your life more meaningful.

Be Totally Committed to your Goals. Whatever you embark upon do it with all of your heart. Invest your whole self in each project. If you cannot make a 100% commitment to a goal, you should come to terms with the fact that it is unattainable. Extraordinary success demands extraordinary commitment.

Always Do your Best. Never make the mistake of thinking that something less than your best will due, it will not. There is an old adage that will forever be true: "Do your best and the best will be returned to you." This is another law of the universe that is immutable. "Use it to your advantage."

Meet the Challenge. This requires discipline and hard work, but doing whatever is required to meet the challenge is exactly what it takes to succeed. There are no short cuts, no side steps, and no cheats.

8. Never Give Up. In the words of Norman Vincent Peale,

author of *The Power of Positive Thinking*, "If you want to get somewhere, you have to know where you want to go, and how to get there, then never, never, never give up!

CHAPTER TWO

Character – Part II

Character counts. Moreover, developing the kind of character that will form the foundation of a life of achievement and success is so vital that we are continuing our discussion of the aggregate features and traits that form a successful human character in this chapter. Habit formation is just another synonym for character development.

Developing Winning Habits

Dictionary.com defines habit as, "an acquired behaviour pattern regularly followed until it has become almost involuntary." Habit is an important building block of character. The formation of good habits – behaviours that become second nature to you – will result in your constantly doing the things that will bring about the desired results.

Extremely successful people sometimes feel that they are just amazingly lucky; that for some unknown reason the universe somehow provides them with what they need to make things work to their benefit. What many of them fail to realise is they have developed a character that has incorporated the features of habit, together with other powerful features that attract success like a magnet.

I wish I could give credit to the unknown author who penned these words:

I am your constant companion.
I am your greatest helper or your heaviest burden.

I will push you onward or drag you down to failure.

I am completely at your command.

Half the things you do, you might just as well turn over to me,

and I will be able to do them quickly and correctly.

I am easily managed; you must merely be firm with me.

Show me exactly how you want something done, and after a few lessons, I will do it automatically.

I am the servant of all great men.

And, alas, of all failures as well.

Those who are great, I have made great.

Those who are failures, I have made failures.

I am not a machine, though I work with all the precision of a machine

Plus, the intelligence of man.

You may run me for profit, or run me for ruin; it makes no difference to me.

Take me, train me, be firm with me and I will put the world at your feet.

Be easy with me, and I will destroy you.

Who am I?

I am a HABIT!

Habits are powerful features of our character. Once established they work automatically to accomplish their intended purpose. They are easily your best friend, or your single greatest enemy in you quest for a successful life.

How long does it take to form a habit? Generally, it takes about three weeks. Not much time to invest in something that will pay you rich dividends for the rest of your life.

Remember, however, that habits are a double-edged sword. We form habits because we are human beings. However, many of the habits we form during our childhood and early adulthood are either neutral or negative habits that will continue to function automatically until we change them. What is worse, until we change them, the negative habits we have formed will continue attracting negative conditions that influence our ability to succeed.

Tyrone Edwards wrote, "Any act often repeated soon forms a habit; and habit allowed steadily gains in strength. At first it may be but a spider's web, easily broken through, but if not resisted it soon binds us with chains of steel." Samuel Johnson expressed the same idea when he wrote, "The chains of habit are generally too weak to be felt, until they are too strong to be broken."

Still another author, whose name is unknown, wrote about the danger of bad habits that subtly attach themselves to our lives. He tells the following story to make his point: "You cannot kill a frog by dropping him into hot water. For when you do, he reacts so quickly that he jumps out unharmed. However, if you put him in cold water and gradually warm it until it is scalding hot, you have him cooked before he knows it. The intrusion of bad habits in our lives is very much like this."

Success and Failure Are Habits

In 1908, a young newspaper reporter by the name of Napoleon Hill interviewed Andrew Carnegie who was then the richest person in the world. Hill spent hours attempting to discover Carnegie's secrets to success. One of the most important secrets learned by Hill that day was later revealed in his book, *How To Raise Your Own Salary*. At one point during their discussion, Hill turned to Carnegie and said, "From what you say about habits, I reach the conclusion that success is a habit." Carnegie replied, "Now you're getting the idea. Success is a habit."

Success becomes a habit when all of our other habits are positive. Later in his life, Napoleon Hill wrote, "All of your successes and failures are the results of habits you have formed."

Take a Habit Inventory

Perhaps the wisest, and richest, man who ever lived was King Solomon. He was a man who knew the importance of habit. In Proverbs 26:11, he wrote, "As a dog returns to his own vomit, so a fool repeats his folly." He was, of course, talking about bad habits, and saying that the repetition of bad habits is just as disgusting as a dog returning to his own vomit.

Why did Solomon use such a strong (and disgusting) image? Because he knew that bad habits keep us from reaching our true potential. He knew that by getting rid of bad habits people immediately open themselves to the best of what life has to offer: success, fulfilment, happiness, and purpose.

Exceptionally successful people are constantly reviewing their habits and changing the ones that are no longer useful. When was the last time you reviewed your habits? Let me suggest that you do it today.

What habits are helping you physically, mentally, and spiritually? What habits are helping you start the day with a good attitude and a feeling of confidence? What habits are preventing you from reaching the potential you know you have?

Make a list of all your habits that are problematic, and then commit yourself to changing them one-by-one. You will be amazed at the difference it will make in your life. Your deliberate change in habits will not only give you a new sense of achievement, but it will give those around you a positive, new impression of you.

There is a wise saying, "If you continue to do the same old things in the same old way, you will get the same old results every day." It has always surprised me that most people do not seem to understand the basic principle behind that saying. They fail, and then instead of changing their approach to the problem or situation, they take the path of least resistance and do the same things that caused their failure the first time around.

Mastering Your Habits

Aristotle said, "We are what we repeatedly do." You change who you are by changing your habits. It is that simple. Exceptionally successful people know the power of this secret, and you should too.

Here are some practical steps that will help you change your habits:

Be Attentive to your habits. What things do you find yourself doing "automatically" each day? What impact is the habit having on you? How is it affecting the lives of others?

What is the payoff? What does the habit provide for you? For example, if you habitually leave the dishes unwashed after the evening meal, what are you doing instead? If you watch television rather than wash dishes, then watching television is the payoff.

What is the consequence? Using the previous example, by leaving the dishes in the sink unwashed, and watching television instead of washing them, the consequence is that the sink remains full of soiled dishes.

Define the real issue. Again, using the example of leaving soiled dishes in the sink in order to watch television; chances are the real issue is not a love for watching television. More likely, the real issue is avoidance of a task you dislike.

How pervasive is the real issue. In other words, what other habits have you formed because of the identified primary issue (avoidance, for example)? Once you have identified the real issue behind your habits you are well on your way to changing them.

Wanting to change. Get emotionally involved with your bad habits. Develop a burning desire to change them. Make it personal because it is personal. Getting emotionally involved with anything we truly want to accomplish in life gives us the steam to keep moving forward, and the commitment to accomplish what we set out to do.

Replace ONE bad habit at a time. Do not attempt to change everything at once. Like most worthwhile goals in life, replacing bad habits with positive ones is best-accomplished one step (habit) at a time. In addition, it is important to remember that habits can change without being eliminated. Replace each habit identified as "bad" with a habit that is "good" – one that accomplishes a positive purpose in your life. For example, if you have identified smoking as a bad habit, you might consider replacing it with a health club membership that could result in better overall fitness, unnumbered health benefits, and a longer life to boot.

Persevere. Do not give up. Yes, there will be times when you will tell yourself that it is just too hard to change your habits. When those moments of weakness occur, remember that any goal this worthwhile is going to have its challenges. Stay the course. Visualise yourself as an exceptionally successful person who achieved your success by doing what was required. Remind yourself that one of the most important steps in building a successful future is replacing bad habits with ones that are positive. One more thing: do not forget to reward yourself along the way. Each time you successfully replace a bad habit with a positive habit treat yourself to something special. Better still, involve your spouse or a friend to join your celebration, and be sure to tell them what you are celebrating, and why. The number of people who will follow your lead to a fuller, richer, and happier life will amaze you.

Integrity

Another core quality of exceptionally successful people is integrity. Integrity is being transparently honest in every area of your life, regardless of whether people are watching, or you are alone.

Integrity is the foundation of character. It is one of the most significant qualities you can develop. Integrity will bring you peace, happiness, and success in every area of your life.

To live a life of integrity is to make a commitment to a set of values, then living a life that is consistent with those values. Mental health professionals call this congruent living. Incongruence develops when one professes one thing, but lives in a much different manner.

Incongruence results in all kinds of mental health issues and is responsible for much of the misery and stress that finally causes people to seek professional help.

Think of how many people profess faithfulness to their spouses, but when they think no one will ever find them out, they cheat. Think of how many people profess absolute honesty in all of their financial transactions, and then cheat on their income tax returns when they think they can get away with it. These are just a few examples of the kinds of incongruence that exists in the lives of so many today, and incongruence always brings with it a damaging form of negativity that will undermine every attempt at success.

We live in an age today when the average person feels that all successful business people are nothing more than crooks in disguise. Nothing could be further from the truth.

The worldwide economic crisis and resulting recession of 2009 was caused by a relatively few greedy business people who were morally bankrupt. They were devoid of integrity and moral fibre. Greed had become their way of life, and greed ultimately caused their downfall.

Each of the exceptionally successful people I know live by a code of absolute integrity. They always treat people with respect and honesty, and they demand the same in return. They are rarely swindled or cheated because there is truth to the adage, "You cannot cheat an honest man."

Integrity not only means being absolutely honest with others, it also means being honest with ourselves. Learn a lesson from Dr. Seuss, "Be who you are and say what you feel, because those who mind don't matter, and those who matter don't mind." Be true to the very best that is in you. By living life in this manner you will soon find that by always being true to yourself, you will never be perceived as being "put on" or false with others.

Give Your Best

People of integrity take pride in all that they do. Quality is a way of life for them. Consistent excellence is what they expect of themselves, and those who work for them. They understand that the finished product is always a personal statement of who and what they are.

Failures have secrets. They would never even think of sharing something of potential value with someone else. Exceptionally successful people, because they are people of integrity, always share their very best with others. They understand that living up to one's potential means giving one's best to others, always.

Get The Best

There are a number of universal laws at work in our daily lives. Like it or not, these laws have been set in motion by our creator and will function until the end of time.

For example, we take the Law of Gravity for granted. Whether or not we acknowledge its presence is of little consequence; it is there. Without gravity, you and I would float off the face of the earth into outer space.

Another important law that is at work in the world is the Law of Sowing and Reaping. Like the Law of Gravity, the Law of Sowing and Reaping, established by God, will operate continuously throughout human history.

The Apostle Paul, writing to the Galatians explained the Law of Sowing and Reaping by saying, "Whatever a man sows, that he will also reap." In other words, every action produces a predictable consequence. For example, if you sow love, you will reap love; if you sow trust, you will reap the trust of others; if you sow discord, you will receive discord in return; if you sow hatred, you will receive hate.

Now apply that law to integrity and see what happens. People of integrity – exceptionally successful people – consistently give their very best, and as a result, they receive the very best from others; they have a burning desire to help others succeed in life, therefore others are consistently helping them to succeed greatly.

Be careful of what you are sowing. You will not sow deceit and reap success any more than you can sow seeds of corn and reap potatoes. The Law of Sowing and Reaping is one of the most important laws of the universe you can learn. It is a dynamic law that can begin changing your life the moment you begin using it to attract the things you need for a successful life.

In the Gospel of Luke, we have the recorded words of Jesus talking about the Law of Sowing and Reaping, "Give and it will be given to you. A good measure, pressed down, shaken together and running over, will be poured into your lap. For with the measure you use, it will be measured to you." In other words, give what it is you need, and you will receive it in abundance.

Understand that it takes time for a seed to take root and grow. We live in a society where instant gratification has become a standard. Sometimes we see people seeding all sorts of negative seeds, and often hurting many people in the process. We wonder whether the Law of Sowing and Reaping was somehow suspended in their lives. We may be tempted to wonder the same thing if we have been faithfully planting good seeds in our lives and have yet to see the harvest.

Listen again to a few words from Saint Paul's Epistle to the Galatians, "Don't be deceived; God is not mocked, for whatever a man sows, that he will also reap . . . And let us not grow weary in well-doing, for in due season we shall reap, if we do not lose heart."

Sowing seeds of negativity (hatred, bitterness, selfishness, and greed) will always return a harvest of the same form of negativity to you. Being a person of integrity, and sowing seeds of honesty, wisdom, trust, helpfulness, kindness, and a sincere interest in the well-being of others will return a harvest of success beyond anything you had ever imagined possible. It is a law.

How to Develop the Characteristic of Integrity

Integrity is a vital feature of character. Use the following ideas to develop a better sense of integrity in your life:

Be transparently honest with yourself and with others. If you are prone to lying or exaggerating, stop. Honesty is not only the best policy, it is an essential element of integrity.

Keep your word. If you cannot be trusted to do what you commit to doing, you cannot be trusted in any other area of your life. Your word is your bond.

Do not underestimate the importance of the "little things" in life. What may not seem very important to you may well be extremely important to someone else. In fact, how we deal with seemingly trivial matters will tell us (and the onlooking world) more about our integrity than how we handle larger matters.

Always act as if someone is watching your every move. Spies know this technique well. When assuming a role that includes a fake persona, spies have learned to remain "in character" even when they are alone. Learn a lesson from a spy. You never know when someone is watching.

Practice the Law of Sowing and Reaping. Make it part of your everyday life. A person of integrity is a person who is always concerned about others, and wants to help them succeed. Build-up the lives of others by sowing integrity and success, and reap an abundant life for yourself. Remember: it is a law of the universe. Practice it.

Own your mistakes. Do not make the mistake of blaming others for what you have done. Integrity demands that you own (and own up to) your mistakes.

Thankfulness

The final core quality of exceptionally successful people is thankfulness. Dietrich Bonhoeffer once wrote, "In ordinary life we hardly realize that we receive a great deal more than we give, and that it is only with gratitude that life becomes rich."

Thankfulness, however, is not simply offering a polite "thank you" when someone gives you something or does something for you. When I use the term thankfulness, what I am really referring to is a deep sense of honest gratitude for our many blessings; I am speaking of the kind of soul-felt gratitude that burns in your chest and brings a tear to the eye.

Thankfulness is a state of mind. It is our interpretation of the circumstances, not the circumstances themselves. Thankfulness remembers the blessings of the past, and looks beyond difficulties of the present by interpreting them in a positive way.

Be Thankful

While the author of the following verses is unknown, its meaning is timeless:

> **Be thankful that you do not already have everything you desire,**
> **If you did, what would there be to look forward to?**

Be thankful when you do not know something
For it gives you the opportunity to learn.

Be thankful for the difficult times.
During those times, you grow.

Be thankful for your limitations
Because they give you opportunities for improvement.

Be thankful for each new challenge
Because it will build your strength and character.

Be thankful for your mistakes
They will teach you valuable lessons.

Be thankful when you are tired and weary
Because it means you have made a difference.

It is easy to be thankful for the good things.
A life of rich fulfilment comes to those who are
also thankful for the setbacks.

GRATITUDE can turn a negative into a positive.
Find a way to be thankful for your troubles
and they can become your blessings.

The opposite of thankfulness is an attitude of entitlement, the idea that one deserves the best – equal or better in quality to what anyone else has, anything less results in whining and complaining.

Entitlement says, "people owe me something," "my employer owes me something," "the government owes me something." There are even those who deeply feel that God owes them something.

The attitude of entitlement is a lie that it is possible to get something for nothing, and it is wrong. There is no such thing as a "free lunch."

As of the date of this writing, however, the attitude of entitlement is rampant throughout the world. Entitlement has been a way of life for too many people for too long.

Too many people have got the mistaken idea that they have an inalienable right to live off the system without contributing one iota to the society that feeds, clothes, shelters, and provides for their every need.

What is more, over the past decade there has emerged a sense of "corporate entitlement" that is unlike anything ever witnessed in a free enterprise democratic economy. The attitude of "corporate entitlement," based entirely on the idea that providing an economic safety net for business is one of the primary functions of government, is at the heart of the economic disaster that is now impacting the economies of the world.

People who wanted homes they could not afford, and corporate mortgage companies that were more than willing to profit from their mistakes, caused the present housing debacle. Both felt entitled to their respective treasure.

Several high placed officers of corporations seeking Federal Bailout funds gave themselves multi-million dollar bonuses after banking the funds. They felt entitled.

Before its fall into oblivion, Merrill Lynch was drowning in a sea of red ink. During this time, John Thain, an executive with the firm, felt entitled to spend $1.2 million redecorating his office.

Common sense dictates that greed coupled with an unappeasable sense of entitlement will ultimately bring any nation to its knees. Unless change occurs quickly, the world not only risks economic bankruptcy, but social and moral bankruptcy as well.

What is true of nations is also true of individuals. The antithesis of thanksgiving is entitlement; and a sense of entitlement ultimately will destroy you.

Living a life of thanksgiving, on the other hand, keeps things real. Gratitude for the blessings God has provided to you (family, friends, talents, abilities, opportunity, goals, dreams, etc.) not only will keep you humble, but also will bring even more blessing from God and humankind. Exceptionally successful people are the first to acknowledge the blessings they have received along the way.

Martin Rinkart was a man of character and faith. Much of his life was lived during the Thirty Years War, a conflict between Protestants and Catholics that claimed about one-third of the German population. During the plague of 1637, he was the only pastor still alive in the town of Eilenburg, Saxony, where over 8,000 people died in just one year. Martin Rinkart buried 4,000 of them.

Each day he did the work of several men, which often left him drained physically and spiritually. However, unlike so many of his contemporaries, Rinkart did not become ill.

Following the plague, a famine spread across the land. Men and women fought in the streets over the dead bodies of cats and birds. So troubled by the human suffering he witnessed, Rinkart shared what little food he had with the hungry and borrowed years in advance against his meagre salary to help provide for the needs of his people. Yet, finally, even those close to him began to turn on him with their misplaced anger.

One night, Martin Rinkart sat alone at his desk before a little stub of a candle and penned the words:

V1. Now thank we all our God, with heart and hands and voices.

Who wondrous things has done, in Whom this world
rejoices;
Who from our mothers' arms has blessed us on our way,
With countless gifts of love, and still is ours today.
V2. Oh, may this bounteous God through all our life be
near us,
With ever joyful hearts and blessed peace to cheer us;
And keep us in His grace, and guide us when perplexed;
And guard us through all ills, in this world, till the next!
V3. All praise and thanks to God the Father now be given,
The Son and Him Who reigns with Them in highest
Heaven;
The one eternal God, Whom earth and Heav'n adore;
For thus it was, is now, and shall be evermore.

This is the kind of thanksgiving that remembers the blessings
of the past, interprets present circumstances in a positive manner,
and looks forward with positive expectation. This is the kind of
thanksgiving that naturally springs from the lips of those with a
winning character.

CHAPTER THREE

Creativity

*"I saw the angel in the marble and carved until
I set him free."*
Michelangelo

The second characteristic of extremely successful people is creativity, that innate ability to think out-of-the-box, to see things differently than most, and to make important connections that others miss. In business situations, this kind of creativity is the stuff that fulfils even the wildest of dreams because it creates and sustains exceptional levels of success. It releases ideas that have values.

In today's rapidly changing world, creativity is becoming a rare commodity. Why is that? Because somewhere between childhood and adulthood we allow others to rob us of that natural sense of creativity which was abundantly present at our birth.

In his best selling book, *A Whack on the Side of the Head*, Roger von Oech recalled a classroom exercise having to do with the measurement of creativity. After teaching for several years, this particular teacher became convinced that somehow almost every child between period of childhood and adolescence lost significant creativity. To test her theory, she devised a simple, but convincing, classroom experiment.

In a classroom filled with high school sophomores, the teacher drew a simple dot on the chalkboard, and then asked the class to identify what it was that she drew. Students answering with the same obvious answer immediately raised their hands: a chalk dot.

The teacher then went to a kindergarten classroom and repeated the same chalkboard drawing. What did they think the teacher had drawn?

Some thought it was the top of a telephone pole. Others said it was a squashed bug, an owl's eye, even a cigar butt. One little boy even said it looked like a rotten egg!

What a difference in perception. There is no question that the sophomores had lost what the kindergarteners still possessed: the ability to look at a thing creatively and understand that there is always more than one answer.

Steve Jobs, one of the most successful people in the world, founder and CEO of Apple Computer says that, "Innovation distinguishes between a leader and a follower." Seldom are the terms "creativity" and "leadership" used in the same sentence by today's business managers. Is it because, unlike Steve Jobs, so many business people today do not understand what these two terms encompass, and the power that results whenever they are combined?

Extremely successful people understand that their abundant success in many ways is attributable to their having learned creativity skills, and reviving the way they looked at the world as a child. This change in paradigm, together with their learned creativity skill-set, has given them the unique advantage of spotting opportunity where others only see problems and difficulty.

As we learned from the kindergarten students in von Oech's book, creativity is not about doing something better than others, it is about perceiving, exploring, thinking, imagining, visualising, and discovering. Creativity is organically linked to intelligence much like a super-charged engine is linked to an automobile. Creativity is the true source of genius.

Creativity is raw energy. A natural, healthy process occurs

whenever people become curious and excited about a process, product, problem, or idea.

It was creativity that drove Gregory Hines, the famous dancer, to turning everyday sounds into tap. Creativity is what led Bill Gates to refuse to accept the limitations of basic programming and triggered him to develop a system that would make otherwise complicated computing applications available to the masses and make computers a vital part of everyday life. Creativity is synonymous with productivity.

Creativity is all about finding new ways of solving perplexing problems and approaching difficult situations. Rather than concentrating on the problem or difficulty, creativity seeks the opportunity hidden in plain sight.

Repeatedly, creativity is simply connecting the dots. In fact, highly creative people often do not see themselves as being creative at all. Because of their openness to new ideas, new perspectives, new paradigms, and new approaches, they are often reticent to take credit because they did not do anything more than visualise the solution. However, it is that inspired vision that sets them apart and enables them to be extremely successful in whatever they do.

The old adage says, "Anyone can sculpt an elephant: first, get a huge block of marble, then simply chip away everything that does not look like an elephant." Using your powers of creativity to visualise solutions to needs, problems, or situations is a powerful way to sculpt an elephant.

Left Brain, Right Brain
"Think left and think right and think low and think high.
Oh, the thinks you can think up if only you try!"
Dr. Seuss

Creative thinking is a right-brain activity that makes use of subjective associative innovation. Creative thinking generates possible solutions to problems in an atmosphere that is devoid of judgement.

The creative thinker's goal is to change concepts and perceptions by creating as many potential solutions as possible. Creative thinking encompasses abilities such as evaluation (sensing and appraising problems, discrepancies, and missing essentials), divergent production (the creative generation of multiple answers to a specific problem), and redefinition (the transformation that occurs because a problem or situation has been defined in a different way). Creative people use this kind of thinking to contemplate implications and project possible responses, difficulties, dangers, and outcomes.

Critical thinking is a left-brain activity that attempts to find the solution to a given problem by using objective linear reasoning. It is factually based, analyses probability, and searches for the correct approach.

Both creative and critical thinking are important skills. However, creativity always transforms the ordinary into the extraordinary. Creativity is what is behind the marketing magic that has people standing in line overnight to watch a motion picture, purchase an iPhone, or get their hands on the newest release of Microsoft Windows. Creativity has propelled people like Bill Gates, Paul Allan, Lee Iacocca, Steve Jobs, Jeff Bezos, and others like them into the realm of extreme success. Creativity can do the same for you.

Creativity: Genetic or Learned

Dr. Teresa Amabile, Head of the Entrepreneurial Management Unit at the Harvard Business School, studies the topics of creativity and innovation from a psychological and learning point of view.

She defines creativity by breaking it into three components: knowledge, creative (or critical) thinking, and motivation.

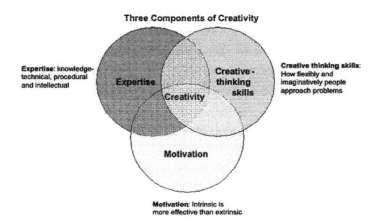

Three Components of Creativity

Expertise: knowledge-technical, procedural and intellectual

Expertise

Creativity

Creative - thinking skills

Creative thinking skills: How flexibly and imaginatively people approach problems

Motivation

Motivation: Intrinsic is more effective than extrinsic

This diagram above is from a thorough report commissioned in 2005 by the National Center on Education and the Economy.

If we accept Dr. Amabile's definition, we begin to discover something of significant interest. While genetics may predispose individuals to certain strengths and weaknesses, learning is the key factor in the development of creativity. Creativity, therefore, is not the exclusive property of a fortunate few, it is something that each of us is able to cultivate in our own lives.

Dr. Edward Glassman also exploded the myth that only a select few people are creative. His research, which included identical twin studies, concluded that rather than being a product of genetics, creativity is a learned skill.

You Can Do It

"But I'm just a common, ordinary person. Are you telling me that I can change my life in positive ways just by learning to be creative?" One of the most asked questions whenever the subject is learning how to be creative. Perhaps it is also your question.

Let me caution you. There is always an abundance of "naysayers" at the introduction of any new idea or concept. Forget them. Do not listen to them. If the great men and women of history had listened to the naysayers of their generations, we would still be in the dark ages.

Then there will be those who will glibly tell you, "If it is not broken, do not fix it!" Do not expect anything original from an echo. These people detest change and those who are bold enough to suggest it. It upsets their status quo.

Pity them, but do not let them sidetrack you on your quest for creativity. These people have long since surrendered their creativity. They will never know the success that you are destined to discover.

I recently heard that the field of psychology has created a new practice specialty that promises to help naysayers. The technical name is psycho ceramics (the study of crackpots). I hope it helps the "naysayer" and the "leave it alone" folks. They certainly are in need of it.

One more bit of advice: Do not ever let anyone convince you that learning how to develop a more creative thought process is something that is beyond your personal reach. There will always be those who believe that creativity is a gift that only a select few possess by virtue of their genetic inheritance, and that the ordinary person cannot possibly learn to be creative. They are wrong. Consider this:

Before they invented the airplane, the Wright brothers were bicycle mechanics. A blacksmith by the name of John Deere invented the first steel plough. Two musicians invented Kodachrome. A self-educated, partially deaf, former train attendant named Thomas Edison invented the electric light bulb (and 1000 other inventions during his lifetime). Each of these giants of history learned how to apply the power of creativity to the needs uncovered by their inquisitive minds.

Like any skill, creativity requires ongoing training and nurturing. However, time spent in the pursuit of growing this skill will reward you beyond your wildest dreams.

Buy good books that discuss creativity skill development; attend seminars on creativity; many universities and colleges now offer courses on developing a personal creativity skill-set. Take advantage of every opportunity to learn more about creativity and learn how to master the skill in your life.

How To Become More Creative

"My alphabet starts with this letter called yuzz.
It's the letter I use to spell yuzz-a-ma-tuzz. You'll be sort of surprised what there is to be found once you go beyond 'Z' and start poking around!"
Dr. Seuss

Creativity gets better and better with practice. The more you "poke around" beyond z, the more fascinating and successful your life will become.

Here are some simple techniques that will help you improve your creativity skills:

Be open to new ideas. Creativity requires that you be open to ideas and concepts that are new even if they seem impossible. Do not simply dismiss what you do not understand. There is no better way to open your mind to new ideas than to try a new task, learn a new skill, or begin a new hobby. You will be amazed at how doing something new will open your mind to new ideas. Suddenly new worlds will open for you.

Be inquisitive. Extremely successful people are always asking questions and seeking answers about better ways of doing things. Curiosity is a way of life for them; it is the hallmark of their success. They are never convinced that anything is as good as it gets. They always believe there is a better, faster, safer, smarter, and more efficient ways of doing things. Never stop being inquisitive.

Revive your childhood curiosity. Never be afraid of asking questions.

Next time you think one of your questions is "silly," remember the questions asked by these creative geniuses:

Leonardo da Vinci once asked, "Why does the thunder last a longer time than that which causes it?" and "Why is the sky blue?"

Socrates asked, "What is beauty?"

Albert Einstein in his youth asked himself, "What would it be like to run beside a beam of light at the speed of light?"

Just think of the inventions that have benefited humanity in countless ways. Most of them came into being because someone answered the simple question, "What if . . . "

Learn to think illogically. Thinking things through logically is something each of us has learned to do. This is how we "process" information in order to make sound, rational decisions.

It is a process however, that excludes creativity. Choose any idea (whether it is yours or someone else's), no matter how illogical it may seem, and begin to think of ways that the impossible might actually happen. Connect ideas and see where it takes you.

Spend time with creative people. You will soon discover that the most consistently creative are children, especially the ones who have been given a box of crayons but have not yet been told to colour within the lines. Their imaginations run wild. They can teach you a priceless lesson: how to think "out-of-the-box."

Quit trying to be perfect. You will never achieve perfection on the earth anyway. There is nothing as inhibiting to creativity as perfectionism. Imperfection is human. Learn to become uninhibited by concern for doing something that is correct. Creativity flourishes in an atmosphere of unconditional acceptance. Creative people are not afraid to be wrong.

Be open. Do not judge creative ideas that come your way no matter how "silly" or "obvious" they may initially seem. Creativity thrives in people with nonjudgemental attitudes. Creative people are tolerant of ambiguity, do not impose boundaries on ideas, and take risks in order to achieve great results.

Sleep improves creativity. In a recent sleep deprivation study conducted by the Sleep Research Laboratory of Loughborough University in Loughborough, UK, scientists using clinically oriented neuropsychological tests found that lack of sleep has a significant impact on creativity. As little as one night of sleep loss has a major affect on innovative thinking and flexible decision-making. Remember what your mother taught you and get a good night's sleep.

Never stop thinking of yourself as creative. Think positively about the fact that you are creative, and that you are becoming even more creative every day. Remember, creativity is learned. The more you learn about it, the more you practise it, the more creative you will become.

Never forget that you have the right to be creative because you were made in the image of God, the Creator of heaven and earth. You are made to be the continuum of His creation.

Amazon.com

"It's not what you look at that matters, it's what you see."
Henry David Thoreau

Jeff Bezos, one of the most creative businesspersons in the world, had an idea that would revolutionize the selling of books. Instead of a typical bookstore with limited space, and dependent entirely upon in-person sales, Bezos envisioned a huge warehouse filled with books of every genre imaginable.

His plan was to sell books exclusively over the internet so that space, location, and the otherwise limited radius of potential customers were no longer factors. Overcoming these obstacles meant that Bezos could sell his books at a much lower cost and gain a tremendous competitive advantage.

The idea had its critics and naysayers, of course. There were those who said that his plan was foolish and that he was little more than a dreamer gone amuck. Today, Amazon.com is the leader in its field.

Creativity is a skill that is important in a competitive world. Learning how to generate new ideas and create new ways to do things will bring you great success in every area of your life. The reality is you could be another Jeff Bezos in the making.

CHAPTER FOUR

Goal Power

"There is one quality which one must possess to win, and that is definiteness of purpose, the knowledge of what one wants, and a burning desire to possess it."
Napoleon Hill

Extremely successful people understand the power of setting goals. Goal setting to them is an everyday occurrence. Goal power is at the very core of their success giving impetus and direction to everything they do.

Goal Power is golden power because it empowers one to turn dreams into reality, and achieve heights that otherwise would have been impossible to attain.

Here is what Goal Power can do for you:

It gives you focus and perspective. Instead of being swayed by the opinions of others, goals give you a sense of course and direction. Remember one of the first lessons you learned in geometry was that the closest distance between two points is a straight line. Goals help you keep moving in a straight line to whatever it is you want to achieve.

You gain encouragement along the way. Part of the goal setting process involves establishing milestones along the way. These milestones are like sub-goals (some people call them objectives). Each milestone reached gives you a sense of achievement and an extra dose of encouragement as you continue on your way toward your ultimate goal.

Goals will direct your actions. They will determine your priorities, and cause you to remain actively involved in situations that will help you achieve your goal.

Establishing goals and implementing a plan for achievement gives you X-ray vision. Well, not really X-ray vision, but certainly enhanced vision to spot opportunities and possibilities you never saw before. Great fortunes have been amassed by some who, while on their way to achieving a goal, found an opportunity that brought them success and happiness.

Setting goals enables you to create your future. If you do not like who you are, where you are, or what you are doing today, goal setting gives you the ability to create a different future. A goal is much like a fresh canvas on which you can design your future reality, and that provides hope.

Using Goal Power is the key to accomplishment. In fact, by living a goal directed life, you will accomplish more in a short time than most others will accomplish in a lifetime.

Take a Lesson from the Turtle

A few weeks ago, I read an interesting little story written by Byron Pulsifer entitled, "What the Turtle Taught Me." I am including it here because I think it teaches some very important lessons about Goal Power.

"Learning is a continuous process of life, and we all learn from different things at different times in life. One of the things that impressed me recently is what I learned from turtles.

"Turtles could teach a vast number of people a lot about reaching goals. For example, have you ever watched a turtle crossing the road, or making their way to a stream? The turtle knows where they are going, in other words, they have set a goal. So what, you ask? Well, the so what is that many people unfortunately go through life with no specific goal in mind. They seem to weave back and forth or do about faces because their life direction seems to change in relation to whatever influences them at the time.

"Turtles, on the other hand, have a set goal in mind easily observed by taking the time to watch them. This turtle has a one-direction mindset knowing that they have to keep going in that direction no matter what. And, no matter how long it takes them, they will do everything they can to reach their objective.

"Sure, the turtle may be slow. Sure, the turtle only has little short legs to get them to their destination. But, the turtle keeps going, and going, and going plodding along. What this turtle is teaching you is that each step it takes, no matter how small, keeps taking it closer and closer to its goal, its ultimate destination. The turtle knows that any action plan is only as good as the path that shows what each step of the action plan will do. And, did you ever see a turtle skip a step, do a leap, break into a run. No. The reason is that turtles have a better sense of the necessity of taking small steps over and over again to reach final victory more than we do.

"The other thing about turtles is that they have a hard shell. The significance of this shell is to help them protect themselves from anything that may attack them. And, as the turtle taught me, we also need to develop a hard shell against those that would want us to fail, that would rather see us fail than succeed because for us to succeed makes them feel uncomfortable since these people want to remain secure in their own less than successful cocoon. Those of us who set out goals to achieve more, to do more, to break out of our comfort zones need to develop a shell that protects us from naysayers, envy, or obstacles that will undoubtedly bombard us as we move forward.

"And, finally, this turtle taught me one main ingredient to

success that rises beyond all others. That is, the turtle, though slow moving, though unable to skip a step, or to rush, told me that the greatest characteristic to possess in reaching a goal is perseverance. No matter what the obstacle, there is a path around it. No matter how many times one is bombarded by negativity, there is strength in conviction. No matter how long it takes, there is a burning desire to achieve. And, through it all, through the entire journey, my ultimate secret weapon is my commitment to persevere. *Thanks turtle.*"

The Power of Desire

Intense desire (passion) is the rocket fuel that propels individuals to meet their goals, whatever they may be. Desire fuels success. Without an intense desire to achieve your goals, you will never be successful. A goal without intense desire to reach it is like attempting to drive a car without fuel. Your intention is good, but without the fuel of desire, you will get nowhere.

Want and desire are two different things. Never confuse them. You and I can want many things, but chances are we really have a passion for a very few.

Many people "want" lots of money. They equate success with money and only money. However, when you ask them why they want lots of money they will respond by saying that they want money so they can drive a big car, live in a big house, have financial security, or have the freedom that only money can provide.

The trouble is that while these people want money, what they really desire is freedom, financial security, living in a big house, and driving a big car. They want money, but they do not desire money.

If it is money you want, then desire it for its own sake. Be comfortable with the car you drive, the house you live in, and the freedoms you now possess.

Think about Warren Buffett, the second richest man in the world with a net worth estimated to be at least $37 billion dollars. He lives in the same house that he bought in 1958 for $31,500. He does not carry a cell phone, does not have a computer at his desk, and drives his own car. He is known for his philanthropy and for his personal frugality.

But Warren Buffett enjoys the game of making money. Ever since he was a youth, he enjoyed the thrill of investing and turning a profit. That thrill ultimately became a burning desire that propelled him to where he is today.

Bill Gates, founder of Microsoft, developed a burning desire to see a computer in every home in the world. That burning desire led him to develop the software necessary to make computer technology available to computer illiterates like me. Bill Gates is now the richest man in the world, but with Gates, money was only a by-product.

Perhaps you have a burning desire to write a book, start a business, become an investor, or do something else of equal proportion. Allow that burning desire to take root and grow within you, but give it structure and definition by setting goals that will help you achieve your dream.

Cultivate your power of desire and achieve whatever it is you truly want in life.

The Power of Decision

Add the power of decision to your burning desire in order to ignite the magic. Consciously decide that you need to do something about the burning desire that lives inside you.

Decide what you will do, how you will do it, and when, and you are on your way. Once these decisions are made, the only thing left to do is act upon them.

Author and speaker Tony Robbins says, "Using the power of

decision gives you the capacity to get past any excuse to change any and every part of your life in an instant." In other words, the barriers that we sometimes use as excuses for failure are all wiped away if we use the power of decision.

I have a friend who worked for a number of years with a criminal population in the State of Wisconsin. He worked with teenagers who had been incarcerated for crimes and who were now being reintegrated into society.

One thing that each of these teens had in common was something called "victimstance," the idea that what they had done was not their fault because someone or something else in their lives had been so horrible to them that they could not help themselves when it came to committing a crime. That was nonsense, and it was his job to teach them otherwise.

You and I have the power of choice. We can decide to be criminals or philanthropists. The choice is ours to make.

But the power of decision is mighty. It will work for us or against us. God has given us a free will along with the ability to choose between what is good for us and what is harmful. Be careful when it comes to the decisions you make. Decisions are what shape and mould your life.

The power of decision also distinguishes a leader. Leaders decide, followers follow. Instead of waiting for things to happen, leaders decide what needs to be done and take action.

Setting goals will do you absolutely no good at all unless you decide to act upon them. Do not be afraid to make decisions with regard to your goals for fear of rejection or disapproval. Take the risk of moving out of your comfort zone to achieve something worthwhile.

The majority of the population today refuses to do that. They want to remain where it is safe and secure, not wanting to move out of their comfort zone, not wanting to take risks of any kind.

But there is a price to pay for this kind of "safety"; it is called submission.

Creating a new reality through goal setting requires the risk of action, and action is the direct result of decision. Determine your goal(s), based upon burning desire, then decide on a program of action. Make the decision to move forward without delay.

I recently read a story written by Ellesse Chow from Goal Setting College (http://www.goal-setting-college.com) about author John Grisham that really drives home the importance of the power of decision. Ellesse writes:

> Out of **John Grisham's** many books, sad to say, I've only read *The Rainmaker*. But that book alone is enough to make a good impression on me because as far as I can remember, he's a very compelling writer. The way he wrote the plot was so captivating that I almost finished it in one day. Yes, it's that good.
>
> Much as I like his writing, I'm pleasantly surprised to know that he took an accounting major in college before he went on to law school and later into full time writing! For those of you who're having qualms whether to make a career switch and set goals for that, perhaps John Grisham's story can bring you some inspiration. Remember, if he can do it, so can you.
>
> **Baseball, Accounting or Law?**
>
> Born to a construction worker and housewife in Jonesboro, Arkansas on 8 February 1955, it was never John Grisham's ambition to be a writer. Instead, like every other boy in his neighbourhood, John was fascinated with baseball. In fact, he was so intrigued with the game that he wanted to be a professional baseball player. To help him fulfill his childhood ambition, when there was an opportunity to play baseball at college level in Mississippi

State University, he took it up earnestly.

However, after reconsidering his prospects, he finally decided that he may not have the necessary attributes to play professional baseball and settled down to focus on his studies. He majored in accounting to prepare for a career as a tax lawyer, although midway, his interest shifted from tax law to criminal law and litigation. After graduating from University of Mississippi Law School, John Grisham practised law in the town of Southhaven, in a firm that brought in small time criminal defendants and personal injury cases, for almost a decade before being elected into the House of Representatives in 1983, in which he served until 1990.

Letting His Imagination Run Wild

As part of the practice in Mississippi, private attorneys are sometimes called to defend clients who are too poor to engage lawyers of their own. It was one of those cases that gave John Grisham his break into a writing career. One day, during the trial of a 12-year-old rape victim, John Grisham started to find himself wondering what would have happened if the child's father decided to take the law into his hands and took revenge by killing her assailants? Using that as a basis, John began writing the plot, juggling his writing in between a 60 - 80 hour workweek. Getting up at 5 every morning, he would work on his amateurish writing for at least an hour before attending to his other official business. After three long years of hard work, his first novel *A Time to Kill* was finally completed in 1987.

Like every other new budding writer, John Grisham faced tremendous challenge when it came to engaging a suitable publisher. Many of the publishers, even 'thirty-something' publishing houses and 'thirty-something' editors rejected his application. Sending one application after another, John Grisham was rejected by 16 publishers before one agent finally signed a contract with him. That agent however, sent him on a wild goose chase by subsequently rejecting his manuscript again. Eventually, it took one editor to give him the exposure that he very much needed. It was none other than Bill Thompson from Wynwood Press, the same editor who discovered Stephen King. He helped John Grisham publish 5,000 copies of his novel and gave him a $15,000 advance.

With the help of the advance, John Grisham bought 1,000 copies of his book and ran a tour in mid South to conduct book signings. Even though the self-financed book tour did not manage to move the title up the best selling charts, this did not dampen his spirit, as he continued to exhibit strong enthusiasm in his writing hobby.

The Much Awaited Break

John Grisham went on to write his second book, about an up and coming young lawyer who joined a superb Memphis law firm that didn't appear to be what it was. It was titled *The Firm*. A short while after he submitted the manuscript to his publisher, he finally got his big break. Paramount pictures quoted $600,000 for the rights to make the plot into a movie! The deal brought strong interest in John Grisham's novel and one of New York's most prestigious publishing houses, Doubleday paid the same amount to purchase the publishing rights for his book. Amazingly, *The Firm* did well to top the New York Times bestseller charts and became the best selling novel in 1991.

Subsequently, John Grisham went on to publish other famous international best sellers such as *The Pelican Brief, The Client, The Chamber, The Rainmaker, The Runaway Jury,*

The Partner, The Street Lawyer, The Testament, The Brethren, A Painted House, Skipping Christmas, The Summons, The King of Torts, Bleachers, The Last Juror, and *The Broker.*

With the income from the sales of his books, John Grisham is now a full time writer and has put his law career on the side. However, John has never regretted his decision to be a lawyer. Because he believed, he owed it to his law career for the inspiration of his many thrilling stories that forms the fundament of his success as a writer today.

What Did I Learn From This Story?

That life may be full of twists and turns and sometimes you'll never know what it may lead you to, but if you learn to equip yourself with the right mindset, you'll be ready when the once-in-a-lifetime opportunity that you've been waiting for manifests. Yes, you too can create your own inspirational story! Here's what I learned:

(1) Be Committed to Your Choices

If you've decided to give up pursuing a dream you no longer have the passion for, give it up totally. Don't harbour any regrets or brood about it. In the case of John Grisham, he gave up a childhood professional baseball player ambition to concentrate on being a tax lawyer before deciding that criminal litigation law was more suitable for him. Despite all those, he was fully committed in his new choices. He would dedicate himself to his new options and fully explore each before moving on to the next. It was that same sense of commitment that allowed him to take out the extra hours in the midst of his tight work schedule to write the novel.

For someone who's not committed in his decision, he'll likely find himself dwelling in the past. Any difficulty experienced after that can easily make him waver. He may end up reverting to the original position where he started.

For example, when I first made the career switch from a financial management to human development, there were instances when thoughts of going back to accounting line cropped back. I was glad I eventually came to terms with it, loving it and stuck with it until the end. In addition, it certainly helped to know that no matter what decisions I made, they were meant for me to grow and not to feel regretful.

(2) Don't Wait for the Break, Create it

When John Grisham was given an opportunity to sell his film rights to Paramount Pictures, a few people may think he's plain lucky.

But I beg to differ. If he didn't plod his way through writing every single page of his first book over the course of 3 years, he wouldn't have the experience of writing, publishing and marketing a book. It was that same experience and his many years of working as a lawyer that laid the foundation for his second book that matched Paramount Pictures' expectations of a blockbuster script.

In my opinion, he didn't wait for that amazing break. His little actions over the years built up to create it.

Many people keep thinking that they always need a big break in order to achieve something remarkable in their lives. So they spend their lifetime waiting – waiting for that golden opportunity when their dreams will be accomplished. Little do they know that the more they wait, the more time they lose. If they had used this time to polish their acting skills before acing that movie role audition, hone their sales techniques before landing that multi-million dollar contract, improve their public speaking presence before making that earth shattering speech, they would have achieved much more than what waiting would give them.

The Powers of Determination and Discipline

Self-discipline and determination are difficult to achieve, but far from impossible.

These powers are products of decision, and present an exercise that strengthens the spirit and the will. These powers will make you impervious to negative situations that might otherwise present roadblocks to your success. They give you the ability to be ready for any challenge or opportunity that happens to present itself on the way to achieving your goals.

The powers of determination and discipline reject the idea of instant gratification in favour of reaching a predetermined goal that it bigger and better. These powers are among the pillars of success and power and possessed by extremely successful people the world over. These powers give you the strength and ability to concentrate all your energy on the goals you are pursuing.

One of the best ways to develop the powers of determination and discipline is to refuse to give in to the unimportant and even unhealthy desires that present themselves to you on a daily basis. When we refuse to give into unimportant desires or temptations, we begin strengthening our powers of determination and discipline.

Author Pinoy Blogger tells an interesting story about the power of determination and discipline that resulted in the building of the Brooklyn Bridge:

> In 1883, a creative engineer named John Roebling was inspired by an idea to build a spectacular bridge connecting New York with the Long Island. However bridge building experts throughout the world thought that this was an impossible feat and told Roebling to forget the idea. It just

could not be done. It was not practical. It had never been done before.

Roebling could not ignore the vision he had in his mind of this bridge. He thought about it all the time and he knew deep in his heart that it could be done. He just had to share the dream with someone else. After much discussion and persuasion he managed to convince his son Washington, an up and coming engineer, that the bridge in fact could be built.

Working together for the first time, the father and son developed concepts of how it could be accomplished and how the obstacles could be overcome. With great excitement and inspiration, and the headiness of a wild challenge before them, they hired their crew and began to build their dream bridge.

The project started well, but when it was only a few months underway a tragic accident on the site took the life of John Roebling. Washington was injured and left with a certain amount of brain damage, which resulted in him not being able to walk or talk or even move.

"We told them so."

"Crazy men and their crazy dreams."

"It`s foolish to chase wild visions."

Everyone had a negative comment to make and felt that the project should be scrapped since the Roeblings were the only ones who knew how the bridge could be built. In spite of his handicap, Washington was never discouraged and still had a burning desire to complete the bridge and his mind was still as sharp as ever.

He tried to inspire and pass on his enthusiasm to some of his friends, but they were too daunted by the task. As he lay on his bed in his hospital room, with the sunlight streaming through the windows, a gentle breeze blew the flimsy white curtains apart and he was able to see the sky and the tops of the trees outside for just a moment.

It seemed that there was a message for him not to give up. Suddenly an idea hit him. All he could do was move one finger and he decided to make the best use of it. By moving this, he slowly developed a code of communication with his wife.

He touched his wife's arm with that finger, indicating to her that he wanted her to call the engineers again. Then he used the same method of tapping her arm to tell the engineers what to do. It seemed foolish but the project was under way again.

For 13 years Washington tapped out his instructions with his finger on his wife's arm, until the bridge was finally completed. Today the spectacular Brooklyn Bridge stands in all its glory as a tribute to the triumph of one man's indomitable spirit and his determination not to be defeated by circumstances. It is also a tribute to the engineers and their team work, and to their faith in a man who was considered mad by half the world. It stands too as a tangible monument to the love and devotion of his wife who for 13 long years patiently decoded the messages of her husband and told the engineers what to do.

Perhaps this is one of the best examples of a never-say-die attitude that overcomes a terrible physical handicap and achieves an impossible goal.

Often when we face obstacles in our day-to-day life, our hurdles seem very small in comparison to what many others have to face. The Brooklyn Bridge shows us that dreams that seem impossible can be realized with determination and persistence, no matter what the odds are.

Getting Started

Much has been said and written about the manner in which goals should be written. Frankly, my advice to you is concentrate on what is important: Write a specific goal, define measurable results and milestones, decide time frames, and create a simple action plan.

Goals in writing become dreams with deadlines. When you write your goals, you take the first step in the process of making your dreams reality.

As Les Brown once said, "Your goals are the road maps that guide you and show you what is possible for your life."

Dream big! Adopt big goals with timelines and action plans. Then see what happens to your life!

CHAPTER FIVE

Turning Adversity Into Opportunity

"Adversity introduces a man to himself."
Author Unknown

Adversity is a common experience each of us shares. Always a life-defining event, adversity shapes our mindset and forms our identity.

Adversity is the occasional pothole in our road to becoming our personal best and discovering our individual destiny. It has the ability to break our axle or awaken us to our surroundings and give us a new perspective on life. The best part is that you, and not the pothole, get to decide the final impact of the encounter.

Adversity can establish and strengthen you, or it can crush you. It can help you become firm and powerful to resist attack and handle any kind of difficulty or it can destroy you. The choice is yours.

Make no mistake, it is often through trials and difficult experiences that success-minded individuals build strength of character, gain confidence, and learn to function as vital members of society. The old Welsh proverb is true: "Adversity brings knowledge, and knowledge wisdom."

Speaking about adversity as a means of character development, the legendary Napoleon Hill, advisor to two presidents of the United States and a friend of the richest and most famous men of the 20th century once said, "The strongest oak tree of the forest is not the one that is protected from the storm and hidden from the sun. It's the one that stands in the open where it is compelled to struggle for its existence against the winds and rains and the scorching sun."

One of the secrets of extremely successful people is that they have learned to become like a strong oak tree by taking advantage of adversity, and the life-defining times that accompany it. They understand that adversity creates wisdom and is the greatest teacher they will ever have.

Extremely successful people have learned a few other things about adversity. For example, they understand that opportunity breeds adversity, and that the more opportunity they gain, the more adversity they will encounter.

This is true even from the standpoint of Christianity. Whenever we ask God to give us a wider range of influence, or greater opportunities to succeed in our chosen calling, we should expect greater adversity to accompany it. That is because God uses adversity to teach us about Himself, to create Christ-like character, and to reveal His unconditional love for us.

Extremely successful people surround themselves with anything that makes them stronger. They understand that with success comes increasing amounts of adversity, and they welcome it. The fear of adversity dissipates quickly when one's perspective and understanding changes. Viewing adversity as something constructive, or possibly even a great blessing in disguise, makes adversity and success part of the same experience.

A Life without Adversity is Like a Classroom Without Lessons

How could you grow without adversity? Think about it. The survivors of hurricane Katrina lived through one of the worst disasters in the history of the United States. Yet they emerged stronger because of the experience, as horrific as it was.

Think of the adversity you have encountered in your lifetime. Did it weaken you or give you strength?

Take a lesson from the monarch butterfly. In attempting to emerge from its cocoon, it endures a long and arduous struggle. It pushes and strains to free itself from the cocoon initially without success. However, the more it works at the problem, the stronger it becomes. Finally, when its wings have gained sufficient strength, it victoriously breaks free of the cocoon and uses its strong wings to fly away.

You are like the monarch whenever you encounter adversity in your life. You will never fly until your wings strengthen, and your adversity (whatever it may be) will give you the opportunity to do just that. What a blessing!

Your attitude is what is important. Your attitude will determine whether your problems will harden you, or whether the blessings they bring with them will shape and mould your life and make you a better person. The old saying is true, "The same furnace that melts gold will also harden clay." You decide.

Stephen Hawking, British theoretical physicist, would not have achieved such popular prominence for his work in the field of cosmology if it had not been for Amyotrophic Lateral Sclerosis, his affliction. In an autobiographical note on the internet Hawking wrote, "Before my condition had been diagnosed, I had been very bored with life. There had not seemed to be anything worth doing. However, shortly after I came out of the hospital . . . I suddenly realised that there were many worthwhile things I could do. I found to my surprise that I was enjoying life in the present more than before . . . it shows that one need not lose hope."

Newton never would have become the scientist he became

had it not been for the bully seated next to him in grammar school. The bully was bigger than Newton, and stronger.

Nevertheless, when Newton tired of being the subject of the bully's constant attention, he mustered his courage and determination and rose up against his adversary whacking his head against the wall of the church. Having defeated him physically, Newton decided to beat him intellectually which he did. In a few days, Newton was at the top of the class. Newton's adversity caused him to muster his internal resources and rise to the occasion. It was a lesson that paid rich dividends throughout Newton's life.

Saint Paul did not use his imprisonments to bemoan his lot in life. Instead, he used his time behind bars to write the fourteen epistles.

Had it not been for the imprisonment of John Bunyan, he would not have authored *Pilgrim's Progress*.

Had Tolstoy not fallen from his horse, the world would never have been blessed with his book, *War and Peace*.

The blind eyes of Helen Keller and Louise Braille brought tremendous improvements in the lives of the blind throughout the world. Their contributions to the blind, and to society-at-large, are enormous.

Jesus gave one of the finest examples of how to live successful lives. He said, "I do not what I will, but that of my Father who sent me". In other words, Jesus lived his life in partnership with the Father in heaven.

Similarly, you need to live your life in much the same manner. Recognise your partnership with God. Do the things you have been given to do, then leave the rest to God.

You will be amazed how much more successful your life will become. During times of adversity, living life in this manner means you can share your burden with God who loves you unconditionally and wants the best possible outcome for your life.

And one additional blessing will be yours: even when the storms of life abound, you will have peace of heart, peace of mind, and peace down deep within your soul. Remember the words of Jesus, "In the world you will have tribulation, but be of good cheer, I have overcome the world."

What a victorious way to live!

Some Christian Principles to Consider

The Psalmist wrote, "Many are the afflictions of the righteous: but the Lord delivers him out of them all." God is our deliverer. Let us never forget that. He will liberate us from whatever adversity may come our way.

However, that does not mean that we have no role in the delivery process. Our role is to do what we can and remain faithful. The Bible gives us some specific instructions for living through adversity:

Be at peace. In the Gospel of John, Jesus shares His last will and testament with us. He knows that His time on earth is about to end. He said, "Peace I leave with you, my peace I give unto you: not as the world gives, give I unto you. Let not your heart be troubled, neither let it be afraid." The Amplified Translation says it this way, "Stop allowing yourself to be agitated and disturbed; and do not permit yourself to be fearful and intimidated and cowardly and unsettled." (John 14:27)

When adversity comes knocking, do not spend your time being afraid, frustrated, depressed, or agitated. All these are a waste of time and energy. Moreover, they display a real lack of trust in God who loves you.

Spend time with God and be strengthened. The Psalmist wrote, "Thou wilt show me the path of life: in thy presence is fullness of joy; at thy right hand there are pleasures forevermore (Psalms 16:11)." Again, "God is our refuge and strength, a very present help in trouble (Psalms 46:1)."

As we spend time with God, we are strengthened. We find a place of refuge and encouragement. This kind of strength that gives us an edge over adversity. As a child of the living God, take full advantage of it.

Do not forget who you are in Christ! The Bible tells you that you are a number of things in Christ: You are a new creation, you are the righteousness of God, you are the workmanship of God, you are more than a conqueror, and you are a child of the living God.

In writing to the Philippians, the Apostle Paul said, "I can do all things through Christ who strengthens me." (Philippians 4:13) That includes any kind of adversity. Just remember who you are, and you will have a renewed sense of confidence.

Be careful about what you say. The Bible says, "A man's belly shall be satisfied with the fruit of his mouth; and with the increase of his lips shall he be filled (Proverbs 18:20)."

Sometimes when we are in the midst of adversity, we tend to lose our cool and say things that we ordinarily would not think of saying. That can be a major problem.

Our words have power. They can bless, or they can curse, make peace or war, build friendships, or create enemies. During times of adversity, they can claim victory in Christ, or they can speak damnation. "Death and life are in the power of the tongue: and they that love it shall eat the fruit thereof." (Proverbs 18:21)

When adversity surrounds you, focus your attention on someone in need. I know, that almost sounds counterproductive. But from personal experience, let me assure you that it is anything but that.

When we are frustrated and upset because of some adversity

in our lives, focusing our time and attention on someone in need is not only kind, it is downright therapeutic. You cannot help someone else and remain preoccupied with your own problems at the same time.

Moreover, when you focus on someone else and offer to help him or her, the law of Sowing and Reaping comes into play in an almost miraculous way. You will find that by helping others, you help yourself. Try it next time adversity strikes your life. The results will amaze you.

Remember the words of Napoleon Hill, "It is literally true that you can succeed best and quickest by helping others to succeed."

Letting Go of Limiting Attitudes and Paradigms

Extremely successful people regularly challenge and defy obstacles in their pathway. They have developed a mindset that is unconquerable and determined. Turning problems into opportunities has become a way of life.

They were not born like this; they became like this on purpose. At some point, these incredibly successful people decided to take their lives to the next level by not fearing failure and by giving all they have to the process of reaching their individual goals.

Each of these great people took inventory of their attitudes and paradigms and decided which ones had to go. Ruthlessly, they got rid of attitudes that were limiting them in some way, and keeping them from moving forward.

It is amazing, but true, that two people born and raised in poverty can achieve two vastly different outcomes. The first person can follow a path of learned helplessness and continue to live a life of scarcity and hardship. The other can believe that they have a date with destiny and that one day they will be rich and famous.

Neither the environment nor their individual situations

caused the difference between the two. It was the difference in their perceptions about themselves and the world around them. The one saw a hostile world that condemned those born in poverty to remain in that condition. The other saw a world filled with opportunity and believed they could achieve whatever they wanted in life.

Oprah Winfrey was born in poverty. Molestation, rape, and physical abuse marred her childhood. Her perception of the world could have been profoundly negatively skewed as a result.

However, Oprah did not see herself as a victim. To the contrary, the horrific experiences of her youth moved her to commit her life to doing whatever she could do to prevent other kids from experiencing the same treatment. In spite of her unfortunate start in life, today Oprah is one of the world's richest and philanthropic women. Not only is she a tremendous role model, but living proof that attitude really is everything.

Limiting beliefs and paradigms are destructive. Let me encourage you to take inventory of your attitudes today and throw out every attitude that limits you in any way. Attitudes like poor self-esteem, thinking of yourself as a victim, helplessness, hopelessness, and others like them do not belong in your life. Get rid of them, permanently, and replace them with can-do attitudes, a thirst to learn new skills, and the confidence of knowing that you "can do all things through Christ who strengthens (you)."

Courage in the Face of Adversity

"You gain strength, courage, and confidence by every experience in which you really stop to look fear in the face . . . You must do the thing that you think you cannot do."

Eleanor Roosevelt

Let me give you a few definitions from the standpoint of the subject at hand. Fear is an emotional response to adversity. It is one of the basic inherent emotions of the human psyche along with joy, sadness, and anger. It can be anticipatory or the response to specific stimuli such as adversity.

In the human being, the innate response to fear is either avoidance or escape. That kind of response is beneficial if you are attempting to avoid an automobile crash, or fleeing from a man with a gun. These, of course, are examples of rational fears that keep us safe from harm and real danger.

However, reacting to irrational fears (like those that accompany adversity) in these ways only serves to increase self-doubt, encourage convenient mediocrity, and prevent you from living a successful, meaningful, and happy life. Irrational fear is really failure in disguise.

Courage is action in the face of irrational fear. It is the bridge between irrational fear and accomplishment. When you courageously face these kinds of fears and work through them, new levels of strength and self-esteem begin to emerge.

Extremely successful people have learned to live courageously in every area of life. They consistently review the choices they make by taking a hard, long look at the assumptions (or excuses) that are motivating them.

They push themselves to live beyond their individual comfort zones by daring to accomplish things that others consider impossible and implementing solutions to problems without a safety net. They do not run away from adversity and the irrational fear that surrounds it, nor do they avoid it. To the contrary, they understand irrational fear for what it is, and embrace adversity confident that through it they will derive great blessing and success.

It is an astonishing fact that our own presuppositions so often determine our outcomes. If, for example, you approach adversity doubting our ability to handle it, we have already surrendered to it. On the other hand, if you understand that success is always at the other side of irrational fear, your perception of the adversity changes, as does your perception of yourself.

Think about it: there are accomplishments that will never be made unless you make them. There are books that will never be written, songs that will never be sung, discoveries that will never be made, problems that will never be solved, inventions that will never benefit humanity, and people whose lives will never be improved unless you have the courage to overcome the irrational fears that surround your greatest opportunities in life.

Dare to overcome. Dare to change your perspectives. Dare to step out of your comfort zone and live boldly. Fortune favors the bold.

Take a tip from the extremely successful: Never let adversity keep you from achieving your dreams.

One Final Word on Adversity

Here are some tips that you should consider implementing today. Do not wait until the next time one of life's storms blows your way. You will be astounded at the difference these simple changes can make in your life and how they will enable you bravely to turn adversity into opportunity.

Erase the negativity: Avoid allowing someone's past experience to influence you in your present situation. So often when adversity strikes, friends and relatives cannot wait to tell you how devastatingly similar our situation is to one they endured. Not meaning to be negative, they tell you how they may never fully recover from their adversity, but hope things go better for you.

Then, as if to add a note of spirituality and hope, they assure you they will keep you in their prayers, (all of which sounds nice but often means they think you will probably not survive the adversity without direct intervention from the Almighty). Combine the negative thoughts expressed by others with the negativity you already feel, and you have a recipe for real disaster.

Whenever you encounter negative words from others, overrule them just as a judge overrules an objection made in court. He simply throws the objection out and warns the jury to disregard it. That is just what you need to do: overrule the negativity and throw it out. "I simply refuse to think that way," is a good response next time someone attempts to plant negative seeds in your life.

Take control of your thoughts and refuse to allow seeds of negativity to take root and grow in your life. Turn them away when they arrive at your mind's front door. Just do not accept delivery. You are, after all, in charge of your thoughts, so take charge.

Remember to look at the Big Picture: Napoleon Hill said, "Whatever the mind of man can conceive and believe it can achieve." Unfortunately, most people confronted with adversity can only envision themselves in the middle of trouble. If they attempt to look forward, they envision only the worst, and never the best, of what the future could hold.

Instead, next time trouble invades your life, keep your eyes on the big picture. Envision a time in your future when whatever the adversity you now face will be past and that it has actually helped you achieve a new level of success. Think about it. Feel it in your being. Keep the vision alive. Let it become so real that it is almost seems like an accomplished fact.

One of the greatest principles in the universe is the Law of Prosperity and Success. This incredible law has stood the test of time, proving repeatedly that we become what we define ourselves to be; we become our own mental picture of ourselves. Think of how amazing that is. Think of the control that gives us in moulding and shaping our lives.

Marcus Aurelius understood that immutable law. He said, "A (person's) life is what their thoughts make it."

Ralph Waldo Emerson understood the law also. He wrote, "A man is what he thinks about all day long."

The Bible also teaches the same truth, "What a (person) thinks in their heart, so do they become." (Proverbs 23:7)

The Law of Prosperity and Success directs that while there are many things in life you cannot decide, your level of success is not one of them.

However, remember, this timeless law is a two-edged sword. By continuing to see yourself as a failure, as someone too inept to deal with life's problems, or as someone who is not smart enough, good looking enough, witty enough, charismatic enough, or worthy enough, you will achieve the status you have envisioned. How you mentally see yourself is a self-fulfilling prophesy.

Do not make the mistake of letting adversity define you. Keep the big picture always in view.

It is as if God has set success and failure before you and asks you to choose which one you want for your life. The ball is in your court. It is up to you.

Use visual reminders of your dreams. You may be wondering how it is possible to create and retain a positive image of yourself and your future. Try this:

Cut out pictures of what your successful life will look like once you have achieved it. Make them colourful pictures of the things that really represent success to you.

Put them up throughout your house, especially in places where you will look at them often. For example, a bathroom mirror is a great place to hang a few of them. Not only can you see the pictures, you can see yourself in the mirror so you can remind yourself that "this is where I'm headed; this is where I want to be."

You will be amazed at how powerful colourful images that

relate to your dreams and goals can inspire you, especially during times of adversity. They will help you to keep you vision positive by making it real.

Welcome to your future. Adversity is part of life, but it does not have the ability to shape your future unless you relinquish that privilege. Your power to determine your future success or failure is awesome.

I sincerely wish I had learned this powerful principle earlier in life. Nevertheless, regardless of age, each of us has something in common. We can determine our success or failure through the simple act of self-definition.

How will you choose to define yourself? Be specific. Do not use general terms combined with general visualisations. It is not enough to say, "I want to be rich and famous . . . or, I want to be the CEO of a major corporation."

Be your own Michelangelo. Be specific about each part of the future you are creating. For example, "I want to be known as a computer applications guru. I want to be one of the top five most knowledgeable people in the world when it comes to my niche. People will beat a pathway to my door just to seek my advice." What definition! That is exciting.

You and I have one more thing in common: Our future begins now. So, where are you headed? How have you chosen to define yourself?

Welcome to your future!

CHAPTER SIX

Developing Skills for Success

Extremely successful people regularly spend time on self-development. They are particularly eager to build skill sets in areas that help them build success in every endeavour they undertake.

Here are their top skill sets:

1. Developing Excellent Interpersonal Skills.

Wikipedia defines interpersonal skills in this manner, "The term 'interpersonal skills' is used often in business contexts to refer to the measure of a person's ability to operate within business organisations through social communication and interactions. Interpersonal skills are how people relate to one another . . . Having positive interpersonal skills increases the productivity in the organisation since the number of conflicts is reduced. In informal situations, it allows communication to be easy and comfortable. People with good interpersonal skills can generally control the feelings that emerge in difficult situations and respond appropriately, instead of being overwhelmed by emotion."

Consider these tips for developing your interpersonal skills:

Do not be egocentric. Recognize the fact that others around you are human beings, just like you. They have ideas, suggestions, and yes perhaps even some criticisms that are valid. Whatever you do, avoid alienating them. Keep your ego in check. Listen and learn from others.

Avoid Negative Talk. Talk positively about everything. Should someone bring up a negative, turn it into a positive if you can. If not, keep your silence.

Do not be afraid to compliment others so long as your compliment is real. A phoney compliment will brand you a phoney, just as negative talk will brand you a negative person. Avoid both like the plague.

Smile. There is nothing more contagious than a smile. Not only can a smile "turn away wrath," as the Bible proclaims, it can also define you as a warm, inviting, and caring person. A smile demonstrates acceptance of those you are with, and they usually will return the compliment with a smile. Likable people smile. Others enjoy helping likable people succeed in whatever they do. The secret of wearing a smile is one of the most important secrets you can learn. Its impact on others is incredible.

2. Developing Leadership Skills

At the age of seven, a young boy and his family were forced out of their home. The boy had to work to support his family. At the age of nine, his mother passed away. When he grew up, the young man was keen to go to law school, but had no education.

At 22, he lost his job as a store clerk. At 23, he ran for state legislature and lost. The same year, he went into business. It failed, leaving him with a debt that took him 17 years to repay. At 27, he had a nervous breakdown.

Two years later, he tried for the post of speaker in his state legislature. He lost. At 31, he was defeated in his attempt to become an elector. By 35, he had been defeated twice while running for Congress. Finally, he did manage to secure a brief term in Congress, but at 39, he lost his re-election bid.

At 41, his four-year-old son died. At 42, he was rejected as a prospective land officer. At 45, he ran for the Senate and lost. Two years later, he lost the vice presidential nomination. At 49, he ran for Senate and lost again.

At 51, he was elected the President of the United States of America.

The man in question: Abraham Lincoln.

Author Unknown

Great leaders are sort of a mystery to most of us. We tend to put them on a pedestal and think of them in mythological ways, as if they were among a select few individuals who were born with the innate ability to lead. Nothing could be farther from the truth.

Great leaders are not born they are made. They are men and women who have not only aspired to leadership, but who also learned the skill sets necessary to become effective leaders.

Do you want to become an exceptional leader? Do you want to possess the vision, self-confidence, wisdom, and motivational ability that extremely successful people have in abundance?

Making a personal decision to learn and develop leadership skills will give you a real advantage as you move toward your goals. These skills will put wheels under you, wings along side you, and propel you to your destination.

Here are some of the most important skills of exceptional leaders:

Exceptional leaders build the self-confidence of those they lead. Unlike mediocre leaders who seem constantly on the prowl seeking others doing something amiss, exceptional leaders are constantly trying to catch people doing something right. Exceptional leaders consider this one of their most important tasks.

Moreover, when they find someone doing something right, they are quick to give them a pat on the back and a verbal commendation. Imagine the impact this kind of heartfelt personal recognition has on members of a team.

Exceptional leaders spend most of their time leading, not managing. Jack Welch was the Chairman and CEO of General Electric Company from 1981-2001. During that time he gained a solid reputation for uncanny business acumen and unique leadership strategies. Welch is an exceptional leader whose innovative leadership styles took a $13 billion dollar corporation and transformed it into a $500 billion dollar corporation during his 20 year career with General Electric.

Jack Welch once said, "We are constantly amazed by how much people will do when they are not told what to do by management." Exceptional leaders understand that in a knowledge-based economy, people need the autonomy to make their own work-related decisions.

Like every exceptional leader, Welch understood that managing less is actually managing better. Bureaucracy, micro-management, and tight control will limit the performance of an individual and kill competitive spirit. In that kind of environment, people do not grow and develop, they are stifled and unhappy.

However people grow, thrive, and prosper in an environment that prizes the individual and views each person as vital with unique gifts and talents to share. This kind of environment builds people up. They become stronger and more committed to the organisation. What is more, they become capable leaders themselves.

Exceptional leaders understand that one of their most important skills for success is their ability to treat people like people, not automatons. They lead by example and by sharing an inspiring vision of the organisation.

3. Teamwork

"Individuals score points, but teams win games."

Zig Ziglar

Exceptional leaders know how to inspire teams to work together. They understand that through this kind of concerted effort they can deliver results faster, better, and more cost effectively.

Someone once said, "The speed of the boss is the speed of the team." If you aspire to be an exceptional leader, remember those words. Exceptional leaders model behaviors of effective leadership and seek to equip their team with the capabilities and skills that, in turn, optimize productivity and performance and result in the delivery of a product or service of extraordinary quality.

Exceptional leaders are not intimidated by the strengths or expertise of individual members of the team. To the contrary, they maintain a work atmosphere in which open and free communication is a fundamental principle. They invite ideas and suggestions from those who are on the front line. These are the people, after all, who know where problems exist and how to solve them.

Teamwork brings a diverse group of people together to focus on a common mission. Getting feedback and suggestions from people who do not all perform the same kind of work will spark the creativity of the team and yield a wealth of continuous quality improvement.

Exceptional leaders hold the bar high. Mediocrity is never acceptable. Products and services that are average or mediocre can always be replaced. The goal is excellence, and that means continuous learning, skill-building, and adapting to meet the challenges of tomorrow.

4. Communication Skills

Exceptional leaders consistently endeavor to strengthen their interpersonal communication skills by building and maintaining open, supportive, and collaborative relationships with others in the organisation. This results in the development of an organisation that has great trust and confidence in its leadership.

It is virtually impossible to be an exceptional leader without first having developed excellent communication skills. These skills will enable you to convey the mission of the organisation as well as your vision as a leader. Consistent communication of these two vital intangibles will ultimately lead to the achievement of both.

On the road to becoming an extremely successful person, make sure you take whatever time you need to become a skilled communicator. Like so many other skills described in this book, communication skills can be learned. However you plan to climb your ladder to success, communication skills will help boost you to the top.

Enroll in a communication course at a community college. Learn the basics of communication and the simple steps to becoming the kind of person that others want to do business with, and others within an organisation want to emulate.

Remember too that listening is an important part of communicating. Research has shown that the average person is a horrible listener, retaining an average of 25-50% of what is being said.

That means that if your boss talks to you for ten minutes giving you instructions on how to complete an important project, you only heard 2½ to 5 minutes of what he was saying. The same is true in family and social situations.

How can you improve your listening habits? Become an "active listener." Active listening is a different approach to listening that immediately improves your level of retention. Active listen skills include concentrating on the speaker while blocking everything else that otherwise might distract you. It means "listening" to body language as well as to what is being said so that you capture the complete message of the speaker. Active listening means participating frequently by asking clarifying questions that help you understand (decode) the real message.

These are simple skills to learn, but their payoff is incredible. Exceptionally successful people are great listeners, and they are always asking questions.

5. Learn how to network.

No one attains success alone. Those who have become part of that elite group of exceptionally successful people have learned how to reach out to others and develop a network of people and resources.

Networking is a "secret" of success that really is no secret at all. Think about someone that you know who has become very successful. Notice how they network. They always seem to be interacting with others, getting their opinions, sharing ideas, talking about projects, inviting collaboration. Learn from them.

Networking is not about the quantity of contacts you make, but it is about the quality of relationships you build along the way. It is about making those vital connections with colleagues, potential employers, as well as peers that will cause them to think about you ahead of others. It can propel your career to heights you never dreamed possible. And, networking is just plain fun. It is an easy and rewarding way to enrich your life and enhance your career.

From a career-building point of view, networking with people face-to-face and person to person is by far the most effective. However, networking (especially social networking) is changing rapidly in our culture.

Networking in our electronic age has taken on a personality of its own. Social networking sites on the internet have literally exploded in terms of usage, and do not make the mistake of thinking that these are all teens. Both Facebook, and MySpace claim to have garnered in excess of 200 million profiles each, with MySpace reporting that only about 25% of users are under 18 years of age. These people use sites like Facebook and MySpace to exchange information about themselves and use blogs and private messaging to communicate with friends and share interests.

Networking is here to stay. Expect significant changes in the way we will do social and business networking in the future. Just remember one important point: Be part of it, or be left behind in the dust.

6. Time Management Skills

Those on their way to the top are busy people. Effective time management skills are essential tools for those aspiring to become extremely successful.

In the busy world in which we live, each of us has too much to accomplish in any given period of time. That is not likely to change any time soon, unless change comes in the form of becoming even busier.

Making the best use of our time is, therefore, not just a good idea, it is essential. Frustration over having too much to do, and too little time to do it, is a sure sign that you are not managing your time effectively. Time management is the pathway to accomplishment.

Let me give you a few time management tips that you can

begin using immediately. You will be amazed at how these few simple suggestions can help you complete tasks quicker and better leaving you more time for other tasks, or just relaxation.

The point is: plan ahead. Take charge of how you will be using your time. Planning is the key. As with so many other things in life, time can either be our benefactor or nemesis, it depends entirely on whether we are willing to control time through planning, or allow time to control, victimize, and frustrate us mercilessly. It is up to you.

Plan your morning the night before. If you work from home, take a few minutes before bedtime to plan what you intend to accomplish the next morning. Make it specific, and write things down in order of priority.

At the office, make it a point to plan tomorrow's schedule before you leave at the end of each workday. To-do lists may seem out-of-date, but they are not. In fact they are exceptionally fine planning tools allowing people to jot down what they want to accomplish tomorrow, in order of priority.

If you have phone calls to make in the morning, look-up telephone numbers the night before and list them together with the names of the people you will be calling. Leave the list by your phone as a reminder.

Schedule some time to be alone each day. Time spent with yourself can be very beneficial. Try finding a place where the likelihood of interruption is remote. Understand that your email and voicemail can take over for a while. This is important time just for you.

This is not time to think about business, or commitments to home and family. This is time spent in quietness and apartness, to gain refreshment and new perspective. If you have a Bible available, read from the Psalms. Renew your mind and refresh your soul at the same time. Do this for fifteen or twenty minutes a day and you will find it to be an oasis in the middle of your workday that renews your strength.

Schedule your most challenging project for your circadian period of peak productivity. Each of us has a period of time during the day when our energy hits its peak. Use that to your advantage.

Some of us are day people. We arise each morning ready to take on the world and defeat whatever gets in our way. Others do not reach their peak energy period until mid-afternoon. The point is if you know when your peak energy period usually takes place, you can schedule you most challenging projects for those times.

There is nothing more frustrating than attempting to "gear-up" for a difficult project when you are at a low ebb. Conversely, working on these same projects during your peak energy period means that you give yourself a real advantage. Projects you thought of as nearly impossible suddenly are cut down to size. Of course, they really have not changed at all. The way in which you are attacking them has changed because you have decided to take control.

Here are a few of the biggest wasters of time. Avoid them like the plague:

1. Procrastination – Putting things off will only lead to frustration and indecision.

2. Crisis Management – This usually is one of the results of procrastination. By putting things off, sooner or later everything becomes a crisis, and all you will find yourself doing is "putting out fires," and that is alright only if you happen to be a fireman.

3. Unanticipated Interruptions – A friend stops by your office to chat about what he and his family plan to do next summer, or to bring you up-to-date on office gossip.

4. Attending too Many Meetings – Especially meetings that do not accomplish anything.

5. Micro-management of Staff – Do this and you rob yourself of a significant amount of time that could be better spent, and you rob your staff of the opportunity to learn and grow.

6. Failure to Delegate – This is not only a tremendous time waster, but a sure way to fail as a leader.

And here are some tips for saving time. Implement them today:

1. Do one task at a time – Multitasking may sound like an impressive buzz word, but it can quickly become a huge time waster. Do one thing at a time. Do it well. Then, move on to the next task.

2. Prioritize your tasks – Attack what is urgent first, what is important next, and what is routine last. I realize there are other more sophisticated methods of prioritization, but start with a simple method and grow into the more sophisticated if you find that necessary.

3. Get rid of busywork – You just do not have time for it. If it must be done, delegate it. If it accomplishes nothing, forget it.

4. Use To Do Lists – Even in the electronic age in which we live, a good old-fashioned "To-Do" list remains one of the best time management tools available. Use it to plan your day, checking off items as they are accomplished.

5. Do not waste other people's time – That just encourages a practice that no organisation can afford.

6. Meetings should have a specific purpose – They should also start on time (everyone present or not), and they should end on time. Late afternoon meetings that are scheduled to end at the end of the workday work well.

7. Get Started – This is without a doubt one of the best tips for managing your time. The natural inclination of most people is to put off starting the first task of the day. If that sounds like you, stop it. When you arrive at the office, start your first task immediately. Not only will this save a significant amount of time, you will find that it inspires and invigorates you to continue the pace.

But in all your time management planning, there is one very important caveat: do not forget to put first things first. Some people spend their entire lives "making a living" but failing to make a life worth living. Do not be one of them.

Stephen Covey in his book, *First Things First*, tells a story that is worthwhile remembering:

> One day an expert in time management was speaking to a group of business students. As he stood in front of the group of high-powered overachievers he said, "Okay, time for a quiz." He then pulled out a one-gallon, wide-mouthed Mason jar and set it on the table. He produced about a dozen fist-sized rocks and carefully placed them one at a time into the jar. When the jar was filled to the top and no more rocks would fit inside, he asked, "Is this jar full?" Everyone in the class said, "Yes." Then he said, "Really?"
>
> He reached under the table and pulled out a bucket of gravel. Then he dumped some gravel in and shook the jar causing it to work down into the space between the big rocks. Then he asked the group once more, "Is the jar full?" By this time the class was on to him. 'Probably not,' one of them answered. "Good!" he replied.
>
> He reached under the table and brought out a bucket of sand and started dumping the sand in the jar until it filled the spaces left between the rocks and the gravel. Once more he asked the question, "Is this jar full?" No!' the class shouted. Once again he said, "Good."
>
> Then he grabbed a pitcher of water and began to pour

it in until the jar was filled to the brim. Then he looked at the class and asked, "What is the point of this illustration?"

One eager beaver raised his hand and said, "The point is, no matter how full your schedule is, if you try really hard you can always fit some more things in it!"

"No," the speaker replied, "that's not the point."

"The truth this illustration teaches us is that if you don't put the big rocks in first, you'll never get them in at all. What are the 'big rocks' in your life? Your children, your loved ones, your education, your dreams, a worthy cause, teaching others, doing things that you love, your health; your mate. Remember to put these BIG ROCKS in first or you'll never get them in at all. If you sweat about the little stuff then you'll fill your life with little things and you'll never have the real quality time you need to spend on the big, important stuff."

So, tonight, or in the morning, when you are reflecting on this short story, ask yourself this question: What are the 'big rocks' in my life? Then, put those in your jar first.

Resolve

Resolve is a skill that every exceptionally successful person possesses in abundance. Resolve is simply refusing to give up, even when the going gets tough. It is a burning desire to achieve a particular goal regardless of the cost.

J. K. Rowling, the creator Harry Potter books is a perfect example of someone with real resolve. She simply refused to give up. Here is a story about J. K. Rowling that demonstrates what resolve did for her:

Harry Potter creator J. K. Rowling might have reached great heights of success but her new lifestyle is a far cry from the world she lived in when she first dreamt up the boy wizard.

In 1990, Rowling's world was rocked when her mother died, aged 45, after a 10-year battle with multiple sclerosis.

She left the UK to teach English in Portugal where she met her first husband, the Portuguese journalist Jorges Arantes, but she continued to write.

In 1993, Rowling gave birth to their daughter Jessica but she split from her hubby soon afterwards and moved to Edinburgh to be near her sister.

She initially intended to start teaching again but dropped the idea because she says she would never have finished the book.

"I knew that full-time teaching, with all the marking and lesson planning, let alone a small daughter to care for single-handedly, would leave me with absolutely no spare time at all," BBC quoted her, as saying.

Living off welfare payments in gritty and depressing government housing, Rowling developed Harry Potter's world as a means of escape.

The author would wander around the town pushing Jessica in a pram until her baby fell asleep, giving her mother the chance to head for a coffee shop to write.

"The owners of her favourite cafe, Nicolson's, would let her stay all day – Jessica sleeping at her side – as she wrote out the stories in longhand, having ordered only a glass of water and an espresso.

"A Scottish Arts Council grant helped her to pay for a typewriter and she hammered out the manuscript, which would eventually convince the publisher Bloomsbury that Potter could be a hit.

"I had to type the whole thing out myself. Sometimes I actually hated the book, even while I loved it," Rowling says on her official website. Harry Potter and the Philosopher's Stone eventually hit the UK shelves in 1997 and then there was no looking back." (ANI)

Micky Jagtiani, at age 20, set out to become an accountant, but his grades were so poor that he left the school he was attending in London. In order to support his family he took a job cleaning hotel rooms and driving cabs in his spare time. Within one year, illness claimed the lives of each member of his family.

Can you imagine the devastation that Micky must have endured? The loneliness and the grief he must have experienced.

However, Micky Jagtiani had resolved to make something of himself. He took what money he had left after burying his family and invested took over a piece of commercial real estate that his brother had leased before dying of cancer.

He started selling baby products. He believed in himself and in his dream. Today he owns one of the most successful chain store enterprises in the Middle East with 280 stores, 6000 employees, and an estimated $650 million in revenues. His net worth is estimated at $2.5 billion dollars.

Ingvar Kamprad, as a young man in Sweden, had a goal to succeed. Although he was born to a humble farm family, he resolved early in life to do whatever was necessary to succeed, and succeed greatly as a retailer. Things were not easy for him especially since he suffered from dyslexia.

He began his journey toward success by selling matches to his neighbours. He would buy matches in bulk from a supplier in Stockholm, and then sell them individually at a low price but a high profit.

When Kamprad was just 17, his father gave him a small sum of money as a reward for academic excellence. Kamprad used that money to begin a small retail business known then, and now, as IKEA.

The I and the K in IKEA stand for Ingvar Kamprad, the E stands for the name of his family farm, Elmtaryd, and the A for a village near his childhood home, Agunnaryd.

Ingvar Kamprad's net worth today is estimated to be in excess of $31 billion dollars.

You also can join these people with right skills set. Have you ever sat down and asked yourself, that you might just be a skill away from living your dream to the fullest? Today is the right time!

CHAPTER SEVEN

Honour: Practice the Art of Becoming

"You must constantly ask yourself these questions: Who am I around? What are they doing to me? What have they got me reading? What have they got me saying? Where do they have me going? What do they have me thinking? And most important, what do they have me becoming? Then ask yourself the big question: Is that okay? Your life does not get better by chance, it gets better by change."
Jim Rohm

Extremely successful people are always "becoming." They are like the universe itself, always changing, forever discovering different layers of truth, at all times transforming themselves to meet the challenges of a new era. Like clay in the Master's hand, they are always en route to becoming a new creation and changing the reality in which they participate.

The Art of Becoming

"Becoming" is an art. It does not happen in an instant. In fact, it is a process that never really ends.

The Greek language in many ways is far superior to ours. There are verb forms in Greek where the action begins at a specific time, but never ends.

Recall Jesus' words, "Ask and it shall be given unto you; seek and you shall find; knock and it shall be opened unto you." The verbs "ask," "seek," and "knock," in the Greek are these kinds of verbs. Their action begins in the present, but never ends. What Jesus in fact was saying is that we are to ask and ask and ask and continue asking; seek and continue seeking; and knock and continue knocking.

"Becoming" should be viewed in the same way. We need to realise that success, like life itself, is a journey that never ends. We are always "becoming," and we live in a world that is fundamentally in a state of "becoming."

Exceptionally successful people understand that everything in life is constantly evolving, including themselves. Moreover, they understand that because of this constant change new areas of opportunity and challenge are constantly being uncovered. Anais Nin, an early 20th century author once said, "Life is a process of becoming, a combination of states we have to go through. Where people fail is that they wish to elect a state and remain in it. This is a kind of death."

Exceptionally successful people also understand that they too are constantly changing, and they understand how that change occurs. They understand that to emerge as a leader in a world of change takes discipline.

That is why they are selective about the people with whom they associate. They are careful about what they read, about what they say, about where they are headed, because they know that the words of Rohm are true: ". . . life does not get better by chance, but by change." They are, therefore, keenly aware of the influences and agents of change that surround them, deliberately choosing only those that will help them become better, stronger, wiser, more insightful, and more positive.

I have always thought that the greatest asset of the exceptionally successful people I know is their ability to use change to their advantage. Face it, you can either be swept along with the changes that take place in a world that is becoming, or you can seek to learn from those changes. On a personal level, you can either ignore the whole process of "becoming" or you can influence that process by the choices you make. It is up to you.

But if you choose to take an active role in the process of your "becoming," you are in for the ride of your life. Your simple recognition of a process that affects all of us, and your understanding that you can impact that process at will, gives you a real boost on your road to success.

What are you "becoming?" Is what you are becoming okay with you? Is it taking you where you want to go? If your answer to any of these questions is "no," it is time to make some changes.

Becoming a Person of Influence

What is the difference between someone who performs their job with excellence, and someone who is committed to making a real difference in their field? Influence. Doing one's job well is an expectation that may lead to increases in pay and promotional opportunities.

But excellence in the performance of one's job is simply the price of admission. To become influential it is necessary to take a step above excellence and determine to make a difference in your company as well as in your field of endeavour.

This may sound like a subtle difference, but it is much more than that. A commitment to making a difference and setting yourself apart keeps you moving forward, gaining influence along the way, unlike others who are content with doing their jobs with excellence.

One way of setting yourself apart and making a real difference is by defining, then living by, a strong moral code. There is nothing quite so impressive as someone who makes decisions, not just because they impact the bottom line, but because they are morally correct.

Let me warn you in advance that there will be times when your moral compass, and the dictates of superiors will conflict. These are the times that will test your mettle. Compromise your values, ignore your moral compass and your influence will diminish overnight. Let people know where you stand and why and your influence will grow.

Building influence within your organisation involves developing a strong network made up of individuals at various levels in the organisation. What makes a network different from a simple list of acquaintances or contacts? A network involves reciprocity.

Some people in your network will help you more than you will help them. Others will receive more help from you than they can provide you. That is the design of a healthy network. Exchange is what is important. Giving and getting. And, the stronger and larger your network becomes, the more influence you will have in your organisation.

As important as it is to build a strong network within your organisation, contributing time, effort, and knowledge to your profession, building a network within an association of professionals outside your organisation has several advantages and ultimately will increase your influence within your profession itself.

Immersing yourself in a professional association will put you in touch with those who face many of the same problems and challenges you face on a daily basis. You will find yourself bringing new ideas and suggestion back to the your organisation that may help truly make a difference.

By taking an active role in a professional association could lead to a leadership position within that organisation, a chance to write for the association magazine, or an opportunity to lead a seminar on a specific topic of professional interest. All of these situations, and more like them, will increase your influence within your company and your chosen profession.

Understanding where you fit in the "big picture" also helps you to become more influential. Why? Because communicating your understanding of the "big picture" means that you are not just someone who understands the specific job you have been given, but who understands where that job fits as part of the overall corporation.

Being able to articulate the mission and goals of the corporation, and communicating just where your job fits in that mix, means that you not only are influential, but a prime candidate for promotion.

Bringing Out The Best in Others

Exceptionally successful people are constantly involved with others, helping them reach their ultimate potential. They understand that helping others "become" all they can be will, in turn, result in their becoming even more successful.

They understand that the Universal Law of Attraction operates whether one believes in it or not. It is like the law of gravity. You cannot see it, but it is constantly at work.

The Law of Attraction teaches that giving away that which you most desire opens the floodgates of success for you. The Bible talks about this same principle in terms of sowing and reaping, and casting bread upon the waters that returns to us in much greater quantity.

I have yet to meet an extremely successful person who was not interested in helping others. Little people have secrets and will not share their ideas for success; extremely successful people will not only share their "secrets" but help you implement them in your life.

Are you using the Universal Law of Attraction in your life? If not, start today. If you want more love in your life, become more loving. If you want more recognition, more assistance in achieving your goals, start helping others to receive these things and see what happens in return.

Ghandi once said, "be the change you wish for the world," and that change will direct your pathway. If you wish success, happiness, joy, and a sense of fulfilment, be that to everyone you meet. That is how you bring out the best in others while at the same time shaping your own "becoming."

Here are a few other tips that will help you get the best out of others:

Be the kind of person who inspires others. Your words are particularly important. Remember words can speak life or death; make sure they speak life.

Praise generously and sincerely. Find something praiseworthy in everyone you meet and remind them of these admirable qualities often.

Look beyond the individual and envision what that individual could become. Helping people to envision their potential is the pathway to greatness. Remember, there really is no such thing as "status quo." Everything is constantly in a state of "becoming."

Pray for others, and let them know you are praying for them. There is power in prayer. Do not forget to unleash that power on behalf of others. Helping individuals recognise their true potential is part of God's plan. Praying for others puts you in partnership with God.

Encourage others to surround themselves with successful people. Teach them the importance of choosing their friends, choosing what they read, choosing where they spend their time, and choosing where they are directing their lives. Share your "secrets" for successful living so that others can achieve everything they are destined to achieve.

The power to change your life for the better, as well as the lives of those around you, depends upon the degree of your influence. Without influence, success is impossible.

I highly recommend reading *Becoming a Person of Influence* by John Maxwell and Jim Dornan. This is without doubt one of the most excellent books ever written on the subject and will help you become a better influencer immediately.

Your ability in this area is critical. Each of us is an influencer in life whether we are famous or not. We are influencers at home, in church, on the playground, participating in social gatherings, and wherever else we interact with people.

One of the foremost goals of exceptionally successful people is to extend their influence as they journey through life as "becomers." Why not join them in this fascinating journey.

CHAPTER EIGHT

The Mayfly Speaks

"The Mayfly never sees the dawn
But once before his end.
To think he's born,
Upon the morn,
Yet not see one again. "
Darren "Gav" Bleuel

Throughout the pages of this book, we have explored the characteristics of extremely successful people and have explored their secrets of the success they enjoy. It is my prayer that you will with courage apply what you have learned from these pages and will implement the ideas and concepts they teach without fail. If you do, your life will never be the same.

Before I conclude the book, let me share one last thought with you. Let me tell you the story of the mayfly, one of the least significant of God's creatures. The Latin name for the Mayfly is *Ephemeroptera*, meaning "short-lived flyer."

The female of the species actually has the shortest life-span of all. It spends more than a year at the bottom of a stream in its aquatic nymph form, and then suddenly one day it emerges from its watery environment and begins to fly. Sadly, it lives for only five minutes.

During its short life-span the female mayfly must mate and lay its eggs back into the water. And, all of that without the benefit of time management training.

Nevertheless, each of us could learn a lesson from the mayfly, because each of us has only a limited amount of time to live the life we have been given by God. Like the mayfly, our primary duty is also to leave a legacy behind.

Because of its limited life-span, the female mayfly can only leave its legacy of eggs in order to perpetuate the species. It has no other option.

But you do.

What will you leave behind? A legacy that will enrich the lives of unnumbered generations yet to be born, or will you be forgotten in just a few generations after your death?

The choice is yours.

Take a lesson from the mayfly. Leave a legacy.

Andrew Carnegie

In 1901, at age 66, Andrew Carnegie had become one of the richest men in the world. He had worked hard, invested wisely, and reaped a harvest of wealth and acclamation. Moreover, he had learned the lesson of the mayfly.

Carnegie shocked the world when he abruptly announced that he was selling all of his holdings in order to spend the rest of his life giving away every penny he had ever earned. For the next 18 years, that is exactly what he did.

In 1911 he wrote, "My chief happiness lies in the thought that even after I pass away, the wealth that came to me to administer as a sacred trust for the good of my fellow men, is to continue to benefit humanity for generations untold." Carnegie's one desire was to leave the world a better place. What a legacy he left behind:

Funded the first medical research facility in America

Funded Carnegie Hall

Established the Carnegie Foundation for the Advancement of Teaching

Built 2,811 Public Libraries

Created the Carnegie Institute of Pittsburgh and the Carnegie Institute of Washington

Founded Carnegie-Mellon University

Created the Carnegie Endowment for World Peace

Created the Carnegie Foundation that still gives away millions of dollars each year.

And, all of this because Andrew Carnegie took a lesson from a lowly mayfly.

God help us all to do likewise.

Always remember that the life you have today is a gift from God and whatever you do with it becomes a gift back to Him.

Live your life to the fullest and die empty!

Tunji Ishola

About Lightspring International

Lightspring is a registered social enterprise in UK committed to bringing the best out of the people who have been disgusted, busted and neglected. The vision was birthed out of a burden for "turning a bruised reed into the rod of strength and a smoking flax to a burning and shining light" Isaiah 42:3. We strongly believe that trapped within everybody is a leader waiting for manifestation. We have made up our mind to be hands of comforts in the midst of discomforts and a new breed of "cruse" without greed in bringing people to the fullness of relevance.

The main vision of lightspring is developing the spirit of excellence (character) in young people and setting standards (creativity) for the world. Our passion is not to establish a building called church but to raise the true church in people and setting them ablaze to manifest the fullness of God everywhere.

OPERATIONAL STATEGIES

Young Leaders' Development

This is a training development for every young leader in ministry and market place, to be developed spiritually, mentally, socially and personally in order to deploy their basic goodness and aroma of Christ effectively to the society and thereby making them a trail blazer and catalyst for change of value.

The main passion is to raise a new breed of leaders without greed and clothed in the garment of transparency and accountability.

Welcome Home Project

This is a NEET (Not in Education, Employment and Training)

responsive programme for children between the age of 15 – 19 years from minority group who have become victim of life. Our approach is to create a conducive atmosphere for them where they can feel loved and be developed to deploy their imprisoned splendour to their society and the world at large.

Our approach is to treat each of them differently and personally using both the training and coaching skills to develop them for life and inspire them to be the best.

Contact:

Please do feel free to contact us for more information and for further resources about what we do and how you can network with us.

Director
Lightspring International
London,
United Kingdom.
Email – info@lightspring.org.uk
Web – www.lightspring.org.uk